INDIA

A JOURNEY THROUGH A HEALING CIVILIZATION

Shashank Mani is a graduate of the Indian Institute of Technology, Delhi, and an MBA from the International Management Institute, Lausanne. He has spent over eighteen years in an international business environment, and has worked with Schlumberger, an oil services company; with Accenture, and as the CEO of a BPO company he founded. He has lived and worked in countries as diverse as North Yemen, Singapore, Scotland, England, Nigeria, Switzerland and India, and has travelled widely in the USA. His literary journey began with writing articles for the *Times of India*, the *Asian Age* and the *International Herald Tribune*.

INDIA

A JOURNEY THROUGH A HEALING CIVILIZATION

Shashank Mani

HarperCollins *Publishers* India
a joint venture with

New Delhi

First published in India in 2007 by
HarperCollins *Publishers* India
a joint venture with
The India Today Group

ISBN 13: 978-81-7223-652-6
ISBN 10: 81-7223-652-2

Second impression, 2007

HarperCollins *Publishers*
1A Hamilton House, Connaught Place, New Delhi 110001, India
77-85 Fulham Palace Road, London W6 8JB, United Kingdom
Hazelton Lanes, 55 Avenue Road, Suite 2900, Toronto, Ontario M5R 3L2
and 1995 Markham Road, Scarborough, Ontario M1B 5M8, Canada
25 Ryde Road, Pymble, Sydney, NSW 2073, Australia
31 View Road, Glenfield, Auckland 10, New Zealand
10 East 53rd Street, New York NY 10022, USA

Typeset in Weiss 12/16
Mindways Design

Printed and bound at
Thomson Press (India) Ltd.

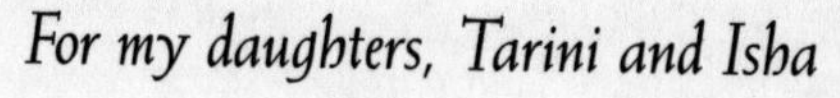

For my daughters, Tarini and Isha

Contents

Preface

In 1997, on the fiftieth anniversary of India's independence, I led a national adventure – the *Azad Bharat Rail Yatra*. This journey, or *yatra*, became an obsession for my wife, Gauri, and me. My whole family, our close circle of friends and many well-wishers joined us in organizing it. The 200 people who participated in the first *yatra* have remained in close contact over the years. This is an extended family forged by the memories of twenty-two days of exhilarating, non-stop travel on a special train. We keep in touch through a web-based forum, and at heart, we remain attached to India. There is a special bond which connects Gauri and me to these participants or *yatris*, and it is this bond that has inspired me to write about our adventure together. These young participants will play a crucial role in keeping the spirit of the journey alive.

Our aim was to discover an India beyond the metros, and their sophistication – an India that was not necessarily fluent in English, but fluent, expressive and observant in its own homespun way. To me, this India was in the smaller towns where I had grown up as the son of an army officer; it was in my town of birth, Gorakhpur, and in Barpar, our ancestral village in the Deoria district of eastern Uttar Pradesh. During our travels, we found that India had several facets. But the central theme that dominated the journey was India integrating with its own genius. For India to compete and prosper in the new world, we must confidently use the talent at our disposal. Participants discovered this first-hand. They celebrated the integrity they saw amongst those they met during our travels. I hope this book offers a similar glimpse to the reader.

What started as a simple story for my daughters and the family took on a more ambitious canvas as I proceeded with writing this book. The book is aimed at Indians who are looking for a positive representation of India and to non-Indians who perceive India as an emerging power. The book, however, is more of a personal essay than a well-researched chronicle. Descriptions of our travels mix freely with our discussions, along with my views on India's future. Our intellectual journey and discussions dominate the book. The reader may find that passion prevails over analysis; a bias for action overtakes observation. Themes of change and entrepreneurship, I hope, remain constant.

One feature of the book is what I call the 'paradox of positivism'. The more we celebrate India's achievements, the less will we be inclined to strive for more. And yet, if we do not applaud our achievements, the positive energy necessary for that forward movement will remain absent. During the journey, we tried to break this paradox by looking at India as a 'glass half-full'. We saw the many seemingly insurmountable problems India faced. We saw cities and villages that could easily be classed as under-developed and poor. We saw the enormous challenges posed by a rapidly growing population and the many divisions India faced across the different regions we visited. But we also noticed the enormous progress India had made in the first fifty years of its freedom. The miracle of a billion strong democracy was worthy of applause. Our blossoming higher education system, even then, was a modern day success story. The judiciary kept our national spine erect. And yet, as we looked ahead, in our fiftieth year of independence, it was clear that we still had some way to go.

Ten years down the line, in India's sixtieth year of independence, the 'paradox of positivism' remains. Headline growth rates, the acquisition of international businesses by Indian companies, a thriving IT services sector, a climbing Sensex, an astronomical rise in property prices and a growing entrepreneurial culture – all reflect India's increasing prosperity. But the paradox should remind us of the dangers of national hubris. The average per capita income even now remains barely above that of Africa. Large parts of India suffer enormous power shortages, our corruption index fails to decline, our infrastructure continues to be patchy, and our institutions are still immature. Yet certain sections of India seem to have declared victory in just the first few stops of this national journey.

The *yatra* explored, and the book argues, that while we have to applaud past success, we have to prepare ourselves for the task ahead. It will be another twenty to thirty years before we can call ourselves a truly developed nation. During our twenty-two-day *yatra*, we recognized that we have to be brave, be willing to take risks, build institutions in order to succeed, but, above all, we have to have the courage to be original. In an era in which computer networks, biotechnology, agri-businesses and environmental issues are reshaping the global developmental agenda, copying an industrial developmental model is a poor recipe for success. Each leg of the journey brought out such themes – whether it was the developmental models discovered in Tilonia, our discussions on China during the visit to Bodh Gaya, the focus on institution-building in Jamshedpur, or the cultural debate in Aurangabad. These themes were brought to life by the *yatris* who led these discussions, and brought their perspectives from different parts of India. The book is structured along those discussions as we travelled through the country. As I think back on our discussions, I find these themes still fresh and surprisingly relevant to India today.

But the relevance of these discussions now extends beyond India. As globalization and technology have made India more visible, so have they offered us a historic opportunity to contribute. In an India where the pursuit of knowledge is equated with the pursuit of wealth and happiness, knowledge has gained new importance. As large parts of the world are beginning to suffer from the first signs of an 'industrial hangover', can India bring in a new developmental perspective? The developmental path we saw being undertaken by some of the pioneering Indians we visited during the journey is bearing fruit ten years down the line. These social, economic and even cultural entrepreneurs are using an original approach to build new institutions, a new India. Can these developmental models show others a new path? Another *yatra*, planned for early 2008, will focus on this new era of change.

I had grown up reading V.S. Naipaul, the Nobel Prize-winning writer and a distant neighbour. A hundred years ago, Naipaul's forefathers left their home near Gorakhpur, in eastern Uttar Pradesh. Naipaul, with an outsider's perspective but an insider's genes, wrote *India: A Wounded Civilization* in 1977, a successor to an earlier book, *An Area of Darkness*. His critique of India and the pervasive cynicism of the time made it fashionable to look upon India as a civilization in decline. His travelogue gave a sense of giving up, a wounded civilization retreating in defeat. He wrote, 'Through centuries of conquest the [Indian] civilization declined into an apparatus for survival, turning away from the mind… and creativity… stripping itself down, like all decaying civilizations, to its magical practices and imprisoning social norms.'

Twenty years later, we too travelled across India, in the company of young Indians who asked similar questions, but with more hope. What we saw was different. But it was different because we observed India with the young Indians who would shape it. Our observations were perhaps more parochial, but more positive as well. If Naipaul wanted to observe and judge, we wanted to observe and change. Our aim was to look towards the future, to discover what is original in India. The journey, we believe, made possible the discovery of a new and positive India, emerging as a leading contender in a world entering the knowledge era – a civilization with the power to heal.

Shashank Mani
26 January 2007

to an ambitious [illegible] of territories [illegible]

or [illegible] all the [illegible]

truth; [illegible] and in important [illegible]

[illegible]

[illegible]

[illegible] but it was different because we

[illegible] with the young [illegible] who would [illegible]

[illegible] were perhaps more [illegible]

[illegible]

[illegible]

what [illegible] The [illegible] people

[illegible] and [illegible] India [illegible]

[illegible] world [illegible] century [illegible]

with the [illegible]

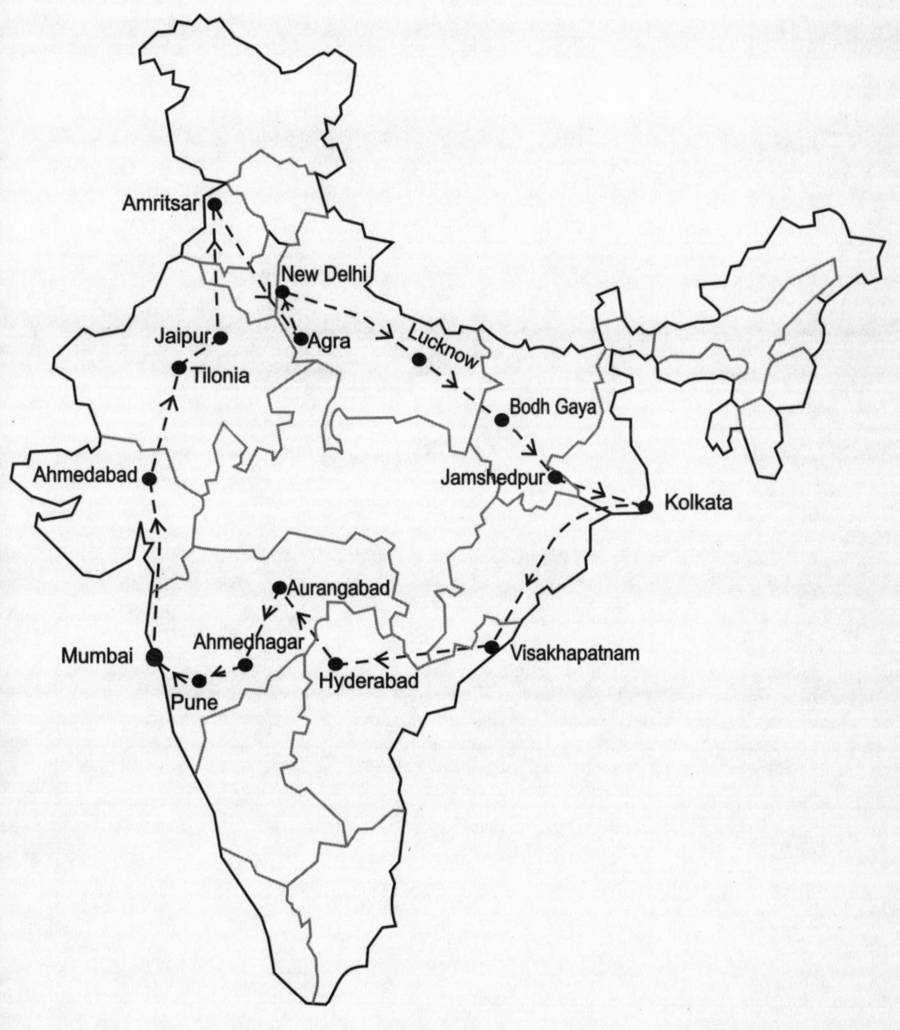

Note: The map is neither accurate nor drawn to scale; it merely depicts the route of the journey.

1

Midnight in Mumbai: The Journey Begins

Thanks to modern technology … history now comes equipped with a fast-forward button.

– Gore Vidal

24 December 1997, an hour before midnight

There was a twinkle in our eyes as candlelight and the sound of Christmas carols lifted our spirits. The 200 of us were looking forward to traversing the length and breadth of India. Our bags were packed, and our minds alert as the train stood waiting. It was approaching midnight, 24 December 1997 as we stood on Mumbai Central railway station; a full fifty years and four months since India gained independence.

I had kept a special *dhoti* for the occasion. It had been kept starched and crisp for some weeks now, and I grabbed it from my suitcase and emerged from the train clad in this cloth of India. By discarding my jeans, and wrapping myself in this *dhoti*, I was making a statement – to myself and to the 200 others – about our true intentions. This journey was bigger than a national adventure, it was our combined attempt to find ourselves.

Once the candles dimmed and the carols were over, we rolled out of Mumbai to look at India afresh. Nine months of preparation and hard work had finally borne fruit. Instead of looking back, we wanted to celebrate the events of 1947 by envisioning a new future.

The participants comprised young students from high schools and colleges across India. Their presence was based on the need to involve youngsters in a project of this nature. We attempted to locate them from all the four corners of India, to represent and inform, as well as to learn from each other. Some participants came from abroad, mainly the UK and USA. They were short-listed through a careful process which analysed their willingness to think differently, and to dream.

Our subliminal inspiration was the Hindi film *Jagriti*. In the film, a teacher takes his young wards on a discovery of India through a train journey, creating an emotional – as well as a physical – bond with the country and its diverse people. I had seen the movie on a small black-and-white television set as a child, but its colourful message of change remained with me.

The project had consumed me for a number of years. Our celebration of the fiftieth anniversary of India's independence in the form of a train journey had a symbolic connotation. The train represented a track into the future, and the young participants represented India's future. The project gave me an energy I had rarely experienced in my corporate career. Gauri, three months into her pregnancy, once she saw how impossibly hard the project was, jumped in to help. Others quickly followed suit. Selling the idea was not a major problem to a group of friends and India-lovers; the execution of the plan was where our true test lay.

Organizing a 10 km trip in India can be a challenge. Selecting and gathering students, then chartering an entire train from the

Indian Railways to travel 7,000 kms across the country was 'madness', as some put it to me during those early days. This was not a simple journey: it involved the logistics of visiting modern institutions, villages and diverse towns in India; getting people who were pathbreakers in their fields on board, and ensuring that the journey had adequate intellectual props to stimulate and excite and, finally, to organize our combined thoughts on India's future.

Our aim was to use the train as a residence on wheels, travelling by night and exploring numerous destinations by day. We had selected fifteen cities and two villages, which would entail circumnavigating the country in twenty-two days. At each stop, we arranged for participants to interact with important dignitaries as well as local students. We wanted to pepper the journey with a discussion on a five-point agenda – population control, agro industries and entrepreneurship, environment and sustainable development, India and the globe; and values.

On a personal level, our journey was inspired by a 'religion of wandering', better expressed in Hindi as *ghumakkadi ka dharma*. As we travelled across the country in its fiftieth year of independence, we were to make our own personal discoveries. We were excited by the sheer thought of a trans-India journey on a special train.

Five months previously, August 1997

It was a non-stop flight to Delhi. At the airport, the immigration officers were more courteous than the last time, as were the customs officials. These were small imperceptible movements in the processes of democracy, tectonic shifts noticed only by those like me who cross these fault-lines regularly. Gurcharan Das's *India*

Unbound had not yet been published, but its message, that India was on the move, as its title indicated, was in the air.

Delhi was a sultry 40°C in the shade. However, for me, as for most returning Indians, the smell of moist grass and dust recently touched by the monsoon was like the welcoming aroma of home food. My driver took me across the expanse of Lutyens' Delhi to Western Court, where I was to stay.

Kranti Shah, the president of the Yuvak Biradari, was also visiting Delhi. Kranti Bhai, as he is known, has devoted his life to this organization he has founded for youth development. Together with his wife, Rekha, he has nurtured the Biradari as an organization that promotes national integration through cultural programmmes. On a good day, he can influence hundreds of young men and women. Today was not a good day.

I tried to persuade him to undertake this journey along with us in this Golden Jubilee year. He informed me that it was too late as he already had a trip planned to the USA. To add to that, we did not have a government grant either. He finally agreed to come with me to the railway ministry, where the route for the special train was being mapped out, and a concession for the students was under consideration.

We had been lobbying with the ministry to grant us the use of the train at special rates. Since students travelling on Indian Railways were eligible for a 50 per cent concession, we argued that this should apply to our venture as well. Our application had been presented twice to the honourable minister, and on both occasions it was rejected. On the second occasion, we were asked by the minister how his state would benefit from this project.

Kranti Bhai and I also tried to muster support from the Maharashtrian stalwart and one-time prime ministerial aspirant,

Sharad Pawar. As we went to meet him at the Parliament House annexe, I gathered that Kranti Bhai's relationship with Sharad Pawar predated our interaction on the *yatra*. The personality of this strong man dominated his small office. Sharad Pawar had cut his political teeth in the sugar cane belt of Maharashtra, specially Baramati, where agri-businesses, horticulture and animal husbandry initiatives have helped provide farmers sustainable models for rural development.

Kranti Bhai and Sharad Pawar chatted briefly in Marathi, and we both talked passionately about the *yatra*, its significance and the reasons why he should help us secure a student concession from the railway minister. Despite the fact that Sharad Pawar was from the wrong state, and at the time belonged to the wrong party, he promised to write to the railway minister. But we knew this to be a kind but futile gesture, given the line taken by the minister earlier.

As all avenues to reach the railway minister were drying up, I took the opportunity to call on ex-prime minister V. P. Singh, best known for his promulgation of the Mandal Report in 1990, which introduced another class of reservation into the Indian statute books. As a result of his singular effort, almost 50 per cent of all government jobs are now reserved in one way or another. He was no longer in power, but as he belonged to the same coalition as the railway minister, he might have had some leverage. I called his secretary and managed to get an appointment with him in New Delhi. As an ex-prime minister, he had a large bungalow in Lutyens' Delhi, though it looked somewhat less whitewashed as the monsoons advanced over North India.

The routine for a visitor was predictable. From the main gate, I was ushered into another internal reception area. Duly registered by a nonchalant Special Protection Group officer, I was shown into another waiting room a few yards away. I waited for an hour – nothing happened. After another hour, I was informed that V.P. Singh was busy and could not meet me after all. I departed despondent and drained, leaving the draft of the letter that needed to be written to the railway minister at the reception.

It was in a state of weariness that I spoke with a friend of my father's, Lieutenant General Shamsher Mehta. He was commanding 2 Corps, and was on a brief visit to Delhi. He is that rare officer who can be cerebral, nuanced, and challenging on a variety of issues. I described the project to him, seeking his support in involving the National Cadet Corps. As he was in Delhi only for a few hours, he asked me to join him in his car at the Army Mess, so that we could chat during the half-hour ride to the airport. Given my weariness, I accepted somewhat reluctantly.

In the state I was in, it took every ounce of energy I could summon to present what we wanted to achieve from the *yatra*. As I spoke, I saw Lieutenant General Mehta's demeanour change. I could see he was excited. Always ready for a new challenge, he leaned forward, and in a tone charged with a passion I will remember for a long time, he said, 'You have to do this!'

I was enthused by his words. My last opportunity was the appointment with the chairman of the railway board, which had been arranged by my father, who was an opposition MP at the time. But that had to wait. The celebrations of the fiftieth year of independence were approaching and I wanted to witness the event first-hand in the Central Hall of Parliament at the stroke of midnight.

The government had made elaborate arrangements to broadcast the speeches of eminent Indian leaders from the Central Hall, exactly fifty years after the 1947 event. Jawaharlal Nehru's famous 'Tryst with Destiny' speech was a natural choice. After some debate in Parliament over the absence of Sardar Patel's speech, Mahatma Gandhi's and Subhash Chandra Bose's speeches were also chosen. As my father had only one additional pass – for my mother – my chances of gaining entry were bleak.

I woke up on 14 August with the certainty of attending only the function organized outside Parliament House on the lawns of India Gate. A number of cultural events were being staged and it seemed half the political and bureaucratic glitterati of India were in attendance. Among the audience, I glimpsed a group of young families, parents and children dressed in the colours of the national flag. It is an image that has stayed with me. They had tricoloured scarves and were waving the Indian flag with no other agenda than their love of India. Their joy was natural, filled with the energy that comes with being the citizens of a young, vibrant and growing nation.

It would take another five years for the national flag to be seen amidst the Indian people. It took the courage of a young businessman from Madhya Pradesh to fight the ban on flying the national flag on any private building. This small but significant step shows how India has evolved. The flag, which in any country should rightfully belong to the people, in India belonged to the government for over half a century. Instead of representing the aspirations of an ordinary citizen – like this family relishing a fiftieth birthday celebration – the flag had come to represent the power of the state, a power which till recently the government used in a manner not too different from the original British administrative setup, which was aloof and imperial.

A fellow MP of my father's had a spare pass. At the last minute, I managed to make my way into the Central Hall of Parliament with the MPs, in time for the midnight ceremony. That is where the spontaneous love and joy for India, seen outside, ended. While ordinary citizens danced outside, inside the president gave an official speech without much emotion. There was a display of emotion only when there was talk of the soldiers guarding our frontiers. Then, Lata Mangeshkar and Bhimsen Joshi – two doyens of Indian music – sang the original version of *Vande Mataram*, which lifted our spirits.

I was prepared for the worst when a few days later my father and I went to meet P. Ravindran, the chairman of the railway board. I was pleasantly surprised when he listened carefully, instantly grasped the intent of the journey, and readily agreed to help. He dictated a letter confirming his support for the journey and asked the respective regional railways to assist, although without any concessions. That letter was flapped more times in front of railway stationmasters in the coming months than anything else he must have written.

Armed with the letter, but not much else, I boarded a flight back to London. I knew that four months was an absurdly short time to organize such a journey. Without a concession from the Indian Railways, we had to raise extra money quickly, as well as take on the logistical challenges of organizing the event long distance. We spoke at Indian venues to solicit funds and generate participation for the journey. We advertised in the *Asian Age*, which was published in London, and created a website that included details of the journey. This later became the portal for candidates wishing to register for the *yatra*.

We approached most of the prominent and not-so-prominent businessmen in London for funds and support. Lord Swraj Paul was courteous and liked the idea; others thought it could give ordinary Britons an insight into a more dynamic India. On the whole, however, we found that for people of Indian origin in the UK, at the time, the idea seemed too far-fetched, too remote.

Azad Shivdasani was an exception. As the head of the Inlaks Group, he runs a conglomerate of companies across the world, but with a heart that firmly resides in India. The Inlaks scholarship, known as the Rhodes scholarship of India, is his family's contribution towards education in India. It sponsors talented young students for a higher education. I had known Azad for over five years when he asked me to help him with new opportunities for his Indian business.

When I approached Azad, he instantly grasped the purpose of the journey. I was asking for funds; he wanted to see commitment. He put me in touch with his friend Ram Gidoomal for support and guidance, and to see whether I would follow through. He promised to give me initial seed funding, but would offer more financial aid only once he had seen substantial progress. In Ram, we found a supporter who was extremely encouraging, as also innovative with his suggestions. Ram subsequently ran for Mayor of London.

Ours was a motley group of organizers, friends and India-lovers from across the world: my friend Somesh Khanna from McKinsey in New York; Madhuvanti Ghose, from the School of Oriental and African Studies (SOAS) London; Vineet Khosla, my friend in Delhi; and finally and most importantly, my father-in-law, Surendra Sharma. Seeing the impossible task we were up against, and gently coaxed by my anxious mother-in-law, he came on board to help. Without him the journey would have been impossible.

In London, the organizing committee would meet at different homes in rotation, even organizing conference calls to give a 'professional feel' to this non-profit venture. Padmini Mahurkar, a friend and supporter, helped us immensely at this stage. When her husband, Monish, a Citibanker, saw us camping in his Putney bungalow on the outskirts of London, discussing the journey and the five-point agenda, his initial incredulity turned into mild fascination, and finally into wholehearted support.

An Australian friend, Steven Yurisich, found the project intriguing and offered to help. I had first met Steven when he had joined Accenture on the same day as I did. Steven came aboard as an organizer in the early days, when no one believed the journey would be possible. He had an instinctive passion for the concept, although he had never been to India. I suspect this endeavour also appealed to his Aussie sense of exploring the Outback. We wanted the journey and the celebrations to extend beyond just Indians. Eventually, thirty non-Indians ended up participating in, and helping, with the event.

In those early days, Steven and I went to the Oxford University Indian student community to drum up support for the *yatra*. We wanted to involve students at Oxford, and so, Steven contacted an Indian student representative at the university. We believed they would naturally feel excited and might get involved. Steven and I took a bus to Oxford after office hours, and strolled along the idyllic streets of the town for our rendezvous at a pub with a small group of Indian students who had agreed to meet us. When we explained the objective of the *yatra* and its nation-building aims, we thought it would strike a chord with them. As the evening wore on, however, Steven remarked how anglicized some of them were. They fitted better into the ancient university town of Oxford than back home in India. While Steven and the students talked further, Steven's hunch was confirmed when there were no real takers for the *yatra*.

Once the initial idea was prepared, I got a glossy brochure printed and waylaid my senior partner, Adrian Lajtha, at Accenture in London. I requested him to help by picking up my mortgage payment for my three-month leave of absence. After a momentary pause, he sanctioned a fully paid leave.

We also wanted to drum up support from North America – the bastion of the Non-Resident Indian (NRI) community. I had a friend at Harvard and wanted to rope in participants and organizers from that prestigious university. I headed out to New York with the brochures. I made my introductions to the Asia Society, to the publisher of *India Abroad*, and to a film company. We also wanted the National Geographic Society and *Newsweek* to cover the event. We even wrote to invite Chelsea Clinton to take part; such was the extent of our ambition.

In the USA, the idea of a trans-India journey found instant appeal. The Indian diaspora identified with the nation-building message of the *yatra*. Samir Seth, an old friend, organized a session at the Harvard Business School which was led by Karthik Muralidharan, an undergraduate student in economics. As we described our project to the students who had gathered in one of the famous semi-circular lecture halls, I could see that Karthik was excited. Though he ultimately was unable take part in the journey, he has become a virtual member of the *yatri* group since then.

I wrote to Victor Menezes, a board member at Citigroup, in an effort to raise funds from New York. John Sequeira, a close friend, knew Victor from India and we felt that he would be supportive. I should have realized that it would require an appointment months in advance to see a top executive in one of the largest banks in the world. But nothing was impossible at that time. I rode the elevator up to the executive suite at the Citigroup headquarters in Manhattan. I knew that getting to formally speak to Victor about our project would be difficult, but if I could 'bump into him' in the corridors, surely he would listen. I managed to linger for a while by talking to his secretary and Victor emerged from the boardroom to find me facing him with my rehearsed two-minute pitch. He was supportive and agreed to help, but being so far removed from India, we were unable to follow up on this conversation.

We were aware of the enormous challenges a country like India faced in its development. Just as the UK and France in the seventeenth and eighteenth centuries, and the USA in the nineteenth century had been forged by a set of guiding principles, India as a young democracy was in search of its own principles. These principles had to be original if India were to succeed in its social and political experiment. Our expedition in this fiftieth year of independence was meant to explore thoughts and ideas that would help shape India's future.

We felt that India was so steeped in history that it did not pay attention to the future. With dramatic changes in society, and with the accelerating pace of technology, history was increasingly a poor guide to what lay ahead. Indeed, for a country where the past is viewed with so many biases, India was better off living in the present and looking ahead to the future.

I had seen how society and its outlook were changing at a pace that surprised even a 'technocrat' like me. When I was posted to Mumbai in 1991, there was a total of two television channels to view. When I left two years later, in 1993, I had trouble choosing from at least twenty channels. Computer education in India has been going through similar growth. Telephones, and more recently mobile phones, are forcing Indian society to look at growth as a non-linear process, as growth in these and some other sectors has been exponential rather than incremental.

To divorce India from its history is not easy. During our research prior to the journey, we found very little – at least in London – that talked of India beyond the days of the Raj. The rest of the world was comfortable with clichés of India as the land of maharajas and snake charmers. Today, India's image is changing rapidly, given the debate over technology and outsourcing in the West, but in 1997, India was a marginal country living up to the Naipaul critique. When we were mapping out a route for our journey, it was with considerable effort that we found an itinerary that would steer clear of 'quaint India' and the palaces recommended by guidebooks. While we took the view that we had to provocatively focus on the future, we knew that the gravity of India's history would pull us somewhere towards a more 'balanced' route. Giving the Taj Mahal a miss would have been difficult, even for us.

India has had to struggle with this unnatural obsession with the past. This was a real and present challenge for us as we tried to organize a *yatra* that was looking towards the future. This remains a general challenge for a country that continues to develop around a fractured view of history. And yet, we were aware that a national identity had to be forged from the glow of the past. The French philosopher Ernest Renan, in his book *What Is a Nation,* has called this 'a plebiscite on whether or not to maintain an existing inheritance and a culmination of a long past of endeavours, sacrifices and devotions'. We wanted this national identity to be forged in modern India. Our aim was to examine what had been achieved over the last fifty years, and what needed to be accomplished in the next fifty.

We sought to build the journey around modern, national institutions and personalities. With the IIT Mumbai convocation hall as our starting point, we intended to visit the Space Applications Centre in Ahmedabad; Tilonia, a village in Rajasthan; the model city of Jamshedpur; and a naval installation on the east coast of India. Our attempt was to instigate a debate on India's future. We wanted to involve young Indians in that debate. In a country where the median age is expected to be twenty-nine by 2025, their participation was important. Involving them in a mass adventure by taking them across the country, meeting progressive Indians and visiting modern institutions would be a life-shaping experience for these young people. Their interactions with local students would enrich both. In this manner, our endeavour would differ from as well as complement other projects in the Golden Jubilee year.

2

North, through Tilonia: In Search of the Original Indian

Be the change.

– Mahatma Gandhi

Thursday, 25 December 1997

As the train made its way north from Mumbai towards Ahmedabad, Vikrant – a participant from Mumbai – stayed awake the entire night. He was penning his thoughts on Mahatma Gandhi. Growing up in the suburbs of Mumbai, he had been inspired by his grandfather, an eminent Gandhian.

Vikrant grew up in a middle-class family, where his parents taught him all the values Gandhi stood for – austerity, truth, honesty and a fearless, undaunted spirit, one that was seemingly gentle but would not yield to pressure. Behind that spirit was a message that seems to have been forgotten: success requires originality and a new approach. While some in the world thought of Gandhi as a half-naked fakir, he used that very nakedness to change the terms of engagement with the outside world. He realized more acutely than others, that in an uneven playing field, the rules of the game had to be changed in order to win. Creative differentiation, not competitive confrontation, was the ticket to freedom. He was the original social and political entrepreneur.

Vikrant had read most of the books written by – as also those about – Gandhi. *The Story of My Experiments with Truth*, Gandhi's autobiography, had influenced him deeply. All night, as we travelled north, Vikrant wrote about Gandhi's life and his true message. As the lights on the train dimmed, the light over his berth burned brightly as he sat thinking about what was relevant in Gandhi's philosophy for India today.

Gandhi's philosophy meant different things to different participants on the train, and indeed to Indians across the country. To many, it signified an outmoded philosophy, in which any form of enjoyment was perceived as wrong. To others, Gandhi was a demi-god who wrested freedom from the British fifty years ago, and was then consumed by the religious passion unleashed by the partition of India. Many in India mocked his philosophy, yet he has maintained his grip on the social structure in India many decades after his death. He helped us achieve independence, yet even his fellow countrymen did not fully understand him. They confused the man with his outward symbols, and lost the larger message of change that he stood for throughout his life.

The train trundled into Ahmedabad on time. There was a quiet anticipation among the participants. It was unclear if the *yatra*, which started punctually, would proceed smoothly. This was also the first test of the various 'mini-systems' we had set up on the train. The shower rooms were still being installed. The sound system was rigged up so that discussions in the common room could be heard by everyone on the train, but it was still rusty. The buses arranged through the Travel Corporation of India (TCI) had arrived, although we were one bus short. A representative of the Space Applications Centre in Ahmedabad was present, but we soon discovered that we were to visit the centre on a holiday. We visited Sabarmati Ashram, home to Mahatma Gandhi, full of mixed emotions: some admired Gandhi and his vision, while others were filled with disdain, or ambiguous about the usefulness of the values he stood for.

The Sabarmati Ashram is where Gandhi spent most of his social and political life in India. Set on the banks of the Sabarmati river, this ashram still houses the small cottage where Gandhi spun yarn, swept the floor, met with visitors, and set into motion the political and social forces that shook the foundations of the British empire. But this was a new generation trying to grasp the ideas of a man who was born more than a hundred years ago, and whose political and social thinking belonged to a different era.

When we asked one of the students to step forward to speak, it was no surprise that Vikrant shouldered forward to take the mike. He poured out his thoughts from the previous night. The importance of Vikrant's pilgrimage to the home of the Mahatma had been amplified by the presence of so many others who were equally keen to understand the true meaning behind his message.

The Mahatma's ability to stand firm in the face of copycat social and economic thinking was Vikrant's central theme. He said that cottage industries were essential for a poor man in a village to live a life of dignity. Vikrant spoke with passion on how developing agro-based industries was the new Gandhian answer for India to prosper in today's world.

Another group on the train was equally positive and passionate about India but wanted to move beyond the Gandhian solution. They argued that in today's India, it would be very difficult to keep villages protected and self-sufficient. Their solution required a mantra that allowed these villages to be integrated into the larger national economy without losing their identity.

Siddharth Desai had served with Gandhi in his early life, and he showed us around the ashram, especially Bapu's hut. We entered the hut with these thoughts in our minds. Inside hung a *kurta* originally worn by Gandhi and spun by him. Vikrant spoke of his desire to be the yarn or *suta* of Gandhi's kurta, to be woven and moulded by the philosophy of Gandhi. Students took turns spinning the *charkha* that was the visible symbol of Gandhi's call for self-sufficiency. The atmosphere in the hut was divided. On the one hand were 'eager weavers', ready to take us back to the days of Gandhi in the 1920s; on the other, was a group that was trying to get us to think afresh on Gandhi's philosophy in order for it to be relevant to India today. Whatever the approach, both sides appreciated the courage, conviction and strength that enabled Gandhi to catalyse change, as also the element of self-awareness that was fundamental to his personality.

Gandhi's protégé, Pandit Jawaharlal Nehru, was far too much a product of the British legacy to be an original thinker in the sense Gandhi was. Educated at Harrow, he returned to India to find the political force of Gandhi's thoughts coursing through the country. He joined in and became part of that struggle, even spinning the *charkha*, but somewhat half-heartedly. Once the influence of Gandhi waned, Nehru copied the Russian model of development – its mechanistic thinking, central planning, and large dams. The opportunity to be original, to look at India and its circumstances in a different light, was not claimed. Worse, in his romantic fascination for the international world, Nehru did not change the systems inherited from the British. In an effort to keep India together, any original thought process was stifled within our democracy.

On the train, we discussed why there had been no conscious efforts to transform our educational and legal systems – indeed most institutions – to cope with the significant economic and social shifts taking place in India and the world at large. Our educational system is still led by rote. Our examination system is still designed to produce clerks. Our legal system copies one which originated in Europe, and was then transplanted to India by the British. Our economic system is still obsessed with things large and industrial. The generation following India's independence was too busy consolidating the nation to pay attention to change and transform these outdated systems. Today, a younger generation is looking to entrepreneurs to lead change, to build and transform the country, economically as well as socially. Much like Gandhi, this generation is adopting differentiation rather than replication as a basis for competition.

From the Sabarmati Ashram, we found our way to the Space Applications Centre in Ahmedabad. During the bus ride through this beautiful city, we admired the buildings of the Indian Institute of Management (IIM), designed by one of the great modern architects, Louis Kahn.

Ahmedabad is a city of can-do entrepreneurs. The Sarabhai family is an example of the intrepid Gujarati spirit with a thousand-year history of trade to back their natural entrepreneurial ability. Vikram Sarabhai – an early pioneer of the space programme – devoted his life to the furtherance of science and space applications. A.P.J. Abdul Kalam, who became president of India in 2002, was Vikram Sarabhai's protégé and talks of building a nation in mission mode.

We arrived at the Space Applications Centre with a sense of anticipation. From Gandhi's simple hut, we were transported into a modern, high-tech auditorium where scientists told us about India's strides into space. Mr Pillai, of the Indian Space Research Organization (ISRO), talked to us about space applications and the role they could play in development – for instance, development could be accelerated with a clear topographic image of the Indian subcontinent. In the dim auditorium, our minds were stirred by the presentations on the Indian National Satellite (INSAT) and the Indian Remote Sensing (IRS) systems that were a part of the space programme.

For us, the scientists and engineers at ISRO were true builders. Starting in a small way, with very basic facilities, they went on to develop satellites that matched those developed by the advanced nations in sophistication and capabilities. The scientists at ISRO and in other strategic sectors, such as nuclear energy, people like Homi Bhabha, Vikram Sarabhai, Brahma Prakash and many others, laid the foundations for the country's scientific development.

However, during this high-tech presentation, our group did not ask any questions. Nor was there a request for an interactive question-and-answer session from the scientists who were making the presentations. This did not augur well for the *yatra*. As we returned to the train, I stood up in the bus and expressed my disappointment. While the scientists and senior staff at the Space Applications Centre deserved respect, the only way the *yatra* would succeed was if the participants engaged in discussion. But another and far more important question lingered in my mind. Would ISRO be able to attract talented young Indians today? Early pioneers like Vikram Sarabhai and Brahma Prakash were exceptional individuals, who by the sheer force of their personality and energy had taken the space programme to new heights. However, could it continue to attract young talent with the same capability and commitment?

We returned to the train that evening emotionally and intellectually charged. Ahmedabad has that effect on you.

I had requested Frank Worth, a well-known documentary director from London, to film the train journey. There had been much protest on this account as our budget was tiny and it was difficult to think of spending additional money on the film. I finally managed to convince the organizing committee that I would personally foot this expense. For me, it would have been tragic not to capture this panoramic journey on film.

I had first met Frank when he accosted me one evening at a presentation in London, where I had been addressing a group about the potential of the journey. He had been born in India, and much of Frank's childhood had been spent touring India as part of a British touring circus. The story he often recounted concerned a week-long trip down the Irrawaddy river to Rangoon as a boy, where he was later escorted by the Army to the safety of the British cantonment. Frank was in love with India. So, he took it upon himself to craft a story for the documentary with two or three participants as his central characters.

Purva Merchant from Pune caught our attention as a possible protagonist for the documentary. She had instinctively taken to the concept of the journey and wrote us an application which impressed the selection committee. In our initial plans, the journey had two legs. We found that Purva's application had pointedly ticked both. She loved her country and had voluntarily made small paper flags which she pinned on participants and passing dignitaries. When I first introduced Purva to Frank, he took a few shots and declared, 'The camera loves her!' And Purva became the central character in the documentary. Thus began the drama of making the documentary: a seventy-two-year-old Frank with limited knowledge of Hindi, coordinated with a camera crew who spoke little or no English, on a moving train where the main protagonist had just been selected and the remaining cast was still to be found!

The cast presented itself from different parts of the world. Devang Patel was studying medicine at the famous Guys and Thomas' Medical School in London. He made it on the journey when a friend dropped out at the last moment. Devang was a young UK-born Asian who had come to India a couple of times before, but this was his first real visit. Around the time Frank discovered him, he was still adjusting to his new environment. As a young person from the other side of the world, he provided the perfect counterpoint to Purva's India-centric views.

Frank then became the comma, full stop, and often exclamation mark for Purva and Devang during the filming of the documentary. In the midst of a full discussion, he would cut in with 'take two'. He was often the first person to walk into a new site on our visits, and very often the last one out, with a tired Purva and Devang in tow. He swung outside the train, took shots from the engine cabin, from the top, and even from the front, having placed himself ahead of the train. He was at his happiest being in India, shooting a group of young people who looked upon him as a father figure.

Frank also managed to invent his own style of 'light' cuisine during the journey. After the first week or so, the oil in the food got to him. So, he started ordering 'lite' meals, which comprised rice, curd, and occasionally, some lentils. Slowly a number of others turned to a similar fare, and I can now admit, sometimes so did I.

Friday, 26 December 1997

When we rolled into Tilonia, a model village in Rajasthan, sharp at 6 a.m., Frank was still in bed. So was the welcoming committee. We had corresponded with the main coordinator at Tilonia, and while our date of arrival had been confirmed, she was apparently still not convinced that such a journey was possible.

Despite the odds, the train emerged out of the fog on time, surprising us and the reception committee. A few observers reported our arrival to those in the village, and a reception party came forth in full force. As the participants started stumbling out of the train, a carnival unfolded on the siding. There were gongs, moustachioed men and *lehenga*-clad women who danced with the participants in a traditional dance of welcome. The colours of Rajasthan and the twirls of the *ghoomar* dance found quick followers among the *yatris*. The welcoming party placed *tilaks* on our foreheads and then walked us to the centre of Tilonia, where Bunker Roy, its founder, was awaiting our arrival. The warmth of that welcome on a misty morning was the first introduction to the India away from the cities for a number of participants.

We entered Bunker's drawing room-cum-office. The room was dimly lit and cool; the floors were covered with a mat. Bunker sat on the floor. He was intrigued by our journey. He was himself a maverick, and the journey appealed to his sense of rebelliousness.

He wanted us to understand what Tilonia stood for and agreed to accompany us on the train journey for a short time to interact with the participants.

Tilonia was founded several years ago by Aruna and Bunker Roy, who wanted to do more for India than be in the administrative service. Together, they built a community in what at the time was a sleepy village, and took an original approach to addressing rural problems in India. Their concept was simple, and broke new ground in village development. They tried to adopt indigenous methods from the village with the help of technology. All the while they ensured that the local population took part in that transformation.

The village had a state-of-the-art water conservation facility – a must in drought-prone Rajasthan. Bunker instituted a series of solar-powered computer rooms for educational purposes; night schools for the children who worked for their parents during the day. The school has a village parliament where the spirit of democracy and suffrage are inculcated in students from an early age. Interestingly, girls as prime ministerial representatives consistently outperform boys in this village parliament.

Tilonia also gave birth to the Barefoot College, whose mission is to train locals for local development. This institution is increasingly finding success across India and the world. The mission of the Barefoot College is to prepare local talent in order to promote village development. Instead of relying on outside or government help, Bunker started mobilizing key locals to address the problems in a self-sufficient manner, by utilizing appropriate technology wherever required. He installed solar-powered lanterns, and trained the locals to work them, thereby ensuring self-sufficiency in electricity. As if just to make this point, as we entered one of the workshops in Tilonia's compound, we saw a woman in a burqa wielding a soldering iron, putting together the circuitry for a solar panel.

We were then taken to the centre of the village, where a welcome speech by the local panchayat of Tilonia had been arranged. The participants wanted to talk to the villagers about the theme of the *yatra*. We wanted to discuss our five-point agenda, our positive aspiration for the future of India, and the aim of the journey. But somewhere before the speech, we fell silent. We recognized that we had to learn from this experience, instead of attempting to impart knowledge. The people of Tilonia understood how to tackle their own situation; all we could do was to absorb their knowledge, experiences and emotions. We would contribute later; now was the time to listen.

After visiting the dams, examining the solar-powered school, and planting trees within the Tilonia complex, a treat was awaiting us. The meal was served on plain banana leaves with the simplest of ingredients. And food has seldom tasted so good. We sat on the floor and slurped down rice, lentils, vegetables and delicious pickle. We were then treated to a puppet show which was used innovatively as a platform by Bunker and his team to spread the message of family planning and women's emancipation. The puppets entertained as well as informed the audience. In the process, the performance also kept alive an art form which was fading away.

To an observer, Bunker could well seem like a Luddite instead of a modern visionary. Modernity to him was not about blindly aping the 'developed' industrial West. He believed that India had done this far too long and had suffered as a result. He maintained that we had to be creative in taking from modern science and technology what was relevant to the Indian reality. In Tilonia, he embraced the solar-powered lamp and solar cell, as well as geodesic domes, and adopted the best practices in terms of water conservation. However, he rejected the educational system – one of whose proponents was Macaulay – left behind from the days of the British Raj. He felt that to create 'a class of persons Indian in colour and blood, but English in tastes and opinions, in morals and intellect' was no longer the best option.

Bunker accompanied us to Jaipur on the train. He spoke in the common room, and asked us whether we were looking for mavericks or conformists. At that time, we were still in the process of discovering our own views. Bunker answered his own question. He believed that breaking the rules, and thinking out of the box, and the creativity required for nation-building needed unconventional thinkers. The mavericks would have to take on the system to change it in their own small way. We were taught by an outdated educational system to be conformists, to maintain the status quo and not to push the institutional boundaries by taking risks. Tilonia was his answer to these nay-sayers. Tilonia was proof that original thinking was not only required, it was the only way for a successful India to emerge.

Since the completion of our journey, Bunker and Aruna Roy have been applauded across the world for innovation in rural development. Around the time we visited Tilonia, they were awarded national prizes by the Jamnalal Bajaj Foundation. Aruna was later given the Ramon Magsaysay Award, and recently Bunker has been applauded by the Prince of Wales Business Leaders International Forum.

Clearly, every success attracts its share of detractors. Some people question the spread of Bunker's message. They see his success limited to Tilonia and its adjoining areas alone. But Bunker has silenced his critics by launching the Barefoot College, which has outposts in different parts of South Asia, as too in South America and in other parts of the world. His message remains the same: use local thinking and talent.

Real progress in India has come from similar original and entrepreneurial bodies in the social and economic sectors. These range from the Self Employed Women's Association (SEWA), Amul, and Grameen Bank in the cooperative sector, to Infosys, Wipro, Suzlon and others in the corporate sector, and numerous other organizations and individuals who continue to work for the betterment of India. These institutions have succeeded in tapping the genius of India that exists in the small towns and villages and not just in the metros, often using English as the link language. A company like Infosys which uses English-speaking IT engineers has grown successfully because its founders believed in the ideal of the frugal and transparent entrepreneur. They then issued stock options to a wide group of employees, involving them in Infosys's growth journey. Azim Premji of Wipro or F.C. Kohli of Tata Consultancy Services (TCS) did not compete by copying successful companies in the USA or Europe. They succeeded because they changed the business model for providing IT services. Bunker has also succeeded in Tilonia because he had the energy to be original.

Bunker bade us goodbye as we arrived in Jaipur, after we spent the evening discussing the visit to Tilonia. Juan Gonsalves – the urban development representative of the Asian Development Bank in Rajasthan – paid us an impromptu visit. In a session in the common room, he spoke eloquently about the problems that urban India faced, where the planning process is often little known and sometimes totally absent. He believed that we have to plan for this mass migration as a large part of rural India finds growing economic opportunities in urban India.

The experience at Tilonia, followed by the talk by Juan Gonsalves, focused the participants' attention on the future villages and cities of India. We decided to add two more topics to our five-point agenda: *azad gaon* and *azad nagar* – two constructs that define the ideal village and the ideal city of the future. This suggestion from the participants was a sign that we were starting to come together as a group.

3

From Jaipur to Amritsar: An Ancient Heritage

The past must be a springboard, not a sofa.

– Harold Macmillan

Saturday, 27 December 1997

The graceful contours of the Pink City beckoned us the next morning from our train windows. The cacophony of a thousand street vendors resounded from the centre of the city. We visited the Amber Fort and then walked around the City Palace in Jaipur. We sat on the side of the pavement, getting *safas* tied to our heads. As we walked back to the palace with bright yellow turbans proudly fluttering in the breeze, the Maharaja of Jaipur, Bhawani Singh, came out to meet the participants. Frank hovered around him, coaxing Purva and Devang into the camera frame.

The visit to Jantar Mantar, the planetarium in the centre of the city, helped channel our discussions. Maharaja Bhawani Singh's forefathers were the architects of the planetarium. Sawai Jai Singh studied ancient texts on astronomy under his guru Jagannatha Samrat, a scholar of both Persian and Sanskrit. Jai Singh asked Samrat to translate the works of Ptolemy and Euclid into Sanskrit, and was inspired by Mirza Beg's observatory in Samarkand. He built four mini observatories in different parts of the country, and once satisfied, moved on to build the Jantar Mantar in 1728, the biggest of them all, right next to his palace in Jaipur. This observatory is still in use for both teaching and calculations. The spirit of scientific enquiry was, however, declining in India, and the Jantar Mantar was emblematic of a past glory. The irony was that the West, meanwhile, was going through an intellectual and scientific renaissance.

Raghav, my friend from college, had come from Australia to visit India at the time. He was looked upon as something of an institution amongst our college fraternity. He has a sharp intellect but alongside that is a heart that is filled with the joy of adventure. We had undertaken a number of trips together during our college days, including the first expedition down the Narmada river on a bamboo raft. Our expedition had a spectacular interlude when our raft hurtled down the Sahastradhara falls with a daredevil Raghav still on board. He had a miraculous escape, and we mended our broken raft to carry on with the expedition. Raghav was in India as this latest adventure loomed ahead and readily agreed when I asked him to join us at least for the first leg of the journey.

Raghav has a particular fondness for Jiddu Krishnamurti, who believed that self-knowledge held the key to transforming the individual, and thereby the world. His teachings had been the subject of much discussion during our college days. Always ready for an existential debate, Raghav's presence brought a philosophical air to the *yatris'* discussions. We debated on the reasons why, despite an early lead in scientific enquiry, India had fallen back in this arena. The answers were varied, ranging from social factors to the broader cycles that lead to the rise and fall of civilizations.

While Sawai Jai Singh was envisioning the observatory at Jantar Mantar the Enlightenment was well under way in Europe. The Enlightenment was an intellectual movement of the seventeenth and eighteenth century Europe in which people started questioning ideas about God, reason, and nature. This instigated a revolutionary movement in art, philosophy and politics. Man started using the power of reason to question the world around him. The movement emphasized the right to self-expression, the right to think freely and express one's views without fear of castigation.

Its starting point was the major scientific discoveries that took place during this period. Johannes Kepler, the German mathematician and astrologer, discovered the first law of planetary motion. Galileo Galilei, the Italian astronomer, developed the first telescope. Francis Bacon, the English philosopher, developed a unique method of reasoning which he called the scientific method. Rene Descartes, the French mathematician and philosopher, considered the father of modern mathematics, revolutionized algebra and geometry. Isaac Newton, the English physicist, mathematician and astronomer, formulated the fundamental laws of gravity and motion.

Apart from developments in science, political and cultural changes were taking place in Europe as well. Overseas exploration led to empires being extended, and the discovery of new corners of the world. Europeans for the first time were introduced to different cultures and a new evolved way of life.

In sharp contrast, India sank further under the yoke of foreign domination. India's intellectual orientation remained intact over the centuries. Philosophy was guided by age-old Vedantic thought. Though western historians often talk of the Vedanta as a mystical philosophy, it is based on an evolved process of the mind. India had a genuine aptitude for cultivating and nurturing knowledge. To be fair, most civilizations have their own heritage of knowledge. China is well known for the institutional knowledge that comes from an unbroken history of political dynasties. India, on the other hand, cultivated and passed on wisdom and knowledge over the centuries. This unbroken chain survived a number of invasions, calamities, religious putsches and assorted rulers.

However, at a certain point in history, India became so dependent on the metaphysical that it lost its direction in the physical world. While adventurers in other civilizations sought new horizons, India curled up on itself and slept. Our vast coastline, which should have seeded great flotillas venturing out to sea, was instead a safe harbour for the Portuguese, the French and the English.

An important economic trend followed this philosophical one – the loss of the entrepreneurial spirit. While particular business groups like the Marwaris, the Parsis, the Jains, the Sindhis continued to lead in business, the wider population remained isolated from commerce. Too much emphasis was given to land tax as a source of government revenue, and far less attention was paid to promoting trade and industry. In large tracts of the North, the transition from agriculture to commerce did not take place in any meaningful manner.

Insights into the 'astonishing collapse' of industrial India in the sixteenth and the seventeenth century may well offer insights to the surprising rise of India in the knowledge economy. Historians have documented the superiority of the Indian industry in the production of textiles, gems and other goods that were the envy of Europe at the time. But this skill was usurped by the disruptive forces of an emergent Europe. While Britain trebled its cotton production between the 1740s and 1770s, in the 'teeming' world of India and China, the cost of labour, relative to that of capital, was too low and industry began to suffer. Today, the situation may have reversed. As new technologies and new knowledge-based skills are growing in demand, a massive re-tooling has to take place in Europe which is proving difficult for an industrial continent.

In contrast, in India, digital communication is transforming the link between knowledge, commerce and industry. Bio-technology is transforming agriculture, food and medicine. India's genius is finding a new field of play. More importantly, as some of these trends are radically new and non-linear, the existing system finds it hard to box, control and stunt them. This has resulted in the emergence of a number of companies and institutions with no restrictive rules. These Indian businesses are spreading across international boundaries at an unprecedented pace. If earlier, the intrepid explorer had to sail into the sunset, now the audacious entrepreneur has the ability to push his service through fibre optics to his customers. This offers a new framework for knowledge and enterprise to be brought together. Instead of being forced to become part of a system that adds little or no value to the nation, Indians can create an environment which respects knowledge, trade, industry and the wealth they create.

We discussed that taking care of oneself had to be matched by focusing on creating something larger than oneself. And even here, an ancient tale from India offers an example. We discussed the parable of King Janak in Indian mythology. When asked by a visiting sage how the honorable raja, living in his opulent palace, could be termed virtuous and 'citizen-friendly', Janak handed the sage a cup brimming with oil. He then asked the sage to walk all around the palace without spilling a drop. If he failed, his punishment would be death by beheading. When the sage returned from his walk around the palace, the king asked him to recount various features of the palace. Nonplussed, the sage replied he was so focused on not spilling the oil that he did not have time to take note. 'Well,' Janak said, 'that is exactly my case. Virtuous leaders are so focused on the task at hand that they can only excel by not thinking about themselves.'

The business writer Jim Collins, in his book *Good to Great*, has similarly highlighted the attributes of what he calls a Level 5 leader. Collins documents the performance of those companies and institutions which were rated 'good' and that over a period of time became 'great'. At the inflexion point, they were led by individuals whom Collins describes as Level 5 leaders. While these individuals were talented and energetic, what characterized them most was a humble focus on the institution or the companies they ran. More than the swashbuckling CEOs who featured on the covers of magazines, these tenacious – often personally reticent leaders – focused single-mindedly on the companies they led, taking their companies' performance from 'good' to 'great'. They were effective because they focused their entire energies and passions on something larger than themselves. They became successful by showing the attributes of a Level 5 leader. Much like King Janak, who was so busy with the welfare of his citizens that he could not describe the wealth of his palace, the Level 5 leader is so focused on his enterprise that he does not have time for personal gratification. For those Indians who wish to excel, the Level 5 model provides an answer. Echoing the values of selfless action, the Level 5 leader is able to forsake personal gain for the greater goal of creating an institution that outlives him or her. In the process, the individual accomplishments of these leaders will lead to a stronger nation, providing a model for many others to emulate their example.

However, we felt that trust and cooperation outside the boundaries of family was lacking in India. Sociologists and writers have offered numerous explanations for the absence of group work in India. One explanation is the division created by caste or class. But that did not surface during our journey, and is conspicuous by its absence in most urban settings, where group work is still not very common. Another explanation, which I believe is closer to the truth, is the lack of abundance. When the national pie is so small, and the bureaucracy makes the process of its distribution even more difficult, cooperation and trust give way to squabbles over who gets the largest slice. The making of an 'integral' Indian, who is rewarded for his hard work and integrity, and works with others in harmony, was the central challenge India faced.

As we made our way back to the train that evening the Pink City pulsated to an old rhythm. As our buses went past the famous Hawa Mahal, I was reminded of the visionaries who had built this city. It had been built according to a plan, rather than allowed to grow haphazardly, and the planning had stood the test of time as the city grew and its population expanded. But the questions put to us by Juan Gonzalves on urban planning kept repeating in my mind. We have to plan well in advance and build new cities with the same vision and originality demonstrated by Jai Singh.

~

Sunday, 28 December 1997

By this time the strain of the journey – a still unsettled train and its youthful but inexperienced organizers – was beginning to show. A few of our facilitators complained that the water ran erratically in some of the washrooms. Others complained that the sound system was inadequate in their compartments. A few organizers, those who had jumped aboard without appreciating the extent of the effort involved in setting up the event, also criticized me personally regarding these matters, though I felt they were minor points if one considered the overall effort involved in organizing the journey.

Raghav and Steven came to my rescue. They asked me to assemble the facilitators in our common room so that I could give them a better understanding of the efforts that had gone into preparing for this trip. It would help bring us closer together as a team. Instead of frittering away their energies complaining about 'water leaks', they ought to roll up their sleeves and get to work.

Until that point, our intention was to keep the 'mundane details' of the journey to ourselves, allowing the participants to focus entirely on the places they visited and the individuals they met. But at this meeting, we decided that the best way of making the journey a success was to involve the participants in the organization of the journey. Raghav and Steven emphatically endorsed this idea, and the others followed suit.

Once everyone had gathered in the common room, I told them the whole story from the beginning, including the difficulties that were faced in getting everyone on board and our financial constraints. They listened attentively as I told them the sequence of events once the organization of the journey shifted to Mumbai from London in September 1997…

In Mumbai, the concept had attracted a number of volunteers. At first in a trickle, and then in a torrent, inquiries poured in. People were intrigued by the concept of the journey, and its forward-looking outlook. Mothers who wanted their children to take part were tempted to be on a trans-India adventure themselves. Fathers, and even grandparents, started enquiring if they could join in. It showed us that the spirit of adventure and exploration was not just for the younger generation.

We established our Mumbai offices close to Kala Ghoda; Raju Shete, a friend, made the arrangements. The train was booked by personal means. However, given that there was no travel concession from the railway ministry, we were in search of a large sponsor. Since it was the first *yatra* of its kind, potential sponsors were not entirely sure that such a journey was possible. As a result, apart from Azad Shivdasani's support, funds collected from friends and family, and a grant under consideration by the Golden Jubilee Committee, we were living in uncertainty.

Different sub-committees were formed to supervise various organizational strands of the journey; the sponsorship committee was headed by me. The selection committee, led by Vrinda Rajgarhia – an old acquaintance in Mumbai – had a panel that examined the applications and considered scholarships for students in need. The public relations group advertised the *yatra* to attract applicants from across the country and tried to rope in dignitaries and eminent Indians to speak and interact with the participants. The journey coordination committee, with Gauri and my sister Shipra in the lead, liaised with the institutions we would be visiting.

We wanted the participants to represent different states of the country. This required that we spread the message of the *yatra* through a number of forums and media outlets. Three individuals –

Ambika Srivastava, Siddharth Kak and Sunil Lulla – helped us at this stage by believing in the nascent journey.

Ambika Srivastava, who at that time was working for McCann Ericsson, saw the potential of the journey and introduced us to a number of corporations and individuals. She also coached us on the selling points of the *yatra*. The journey and its message were close to her heart, and she was the first to believe in the concept in India, and maintained her support even after the event. Siddharth Kak of *Surabhi* had established his television programme with a focus on unusual destinations, illustrating unique Indian experiences. *Surabhi* had a large national following. It popularized Indian art and culture, hoping to rekindle a fascination for exploring the real India. When I went to meet Siddharth, he agreed to publicize our project on his programme, which got us several candidates, particularly from the North-East.

Sunil Lulla at MTV India instinctively understood that this endeavour would appeal to young Indians. He authorized a small video clip describing the journey to be aired on MTV with an invitation for viewers to participate in the event. He was in the midst of transforming MTV into an India-centric channel, and the train journey caught his attention. MTV screened shots of a train making a trans-India journey and this helped us to reach out to young Indians.

India Today, Outlook, Dainik Jagran, Pioneer, Ananda Vikatan and regional periodicals also gave coverage to our project. IPAN, a PR agency, took up our cause and generated considerable press coverage. We were getting an increasingly strong response from participants from all over India.

But the patron saint of our participation awareness effort has to be the writer and journalist Jerry Pinto. He was introduced to us by Dina Vakil, the editor of the *Times of India*, Mumbai. Though initially somewhat sceptical of the journey, he agreed to run a nation-wide story on us in the newspaper's Sunday edition. A photograph was hastily shot with some of the participants at the Mumbai railway station standing against the backdrop of a train. Jerry then put his literary talents to good effect. He also slipped in our contact details and home phone numbers in Mumbai at the end of his article.

That Sunday morning, 6 a.m. onwards, my mother-in-law woke up to a telephonic deluge. It was as if half of India wanted to take part in the journey. The calls would not stop coming. As we put the phone down, it would start ringing again. For over three days, the phone literally did not stop ringing, and calls kept coming for weeks. Participants called from Nainital, Imphal, Hyderabad, and from many other far-flung places. My nephew, Anshuman, all of four, also stepped forward to help meet the challenge. As we noted down addresses in order to send out applications, he helped in the arduous process of sticking stamps as we sent out forms.

We posted application forms to potential participants that included a section for a short essay on their vision for the future of India. The selection panel would then vet them and a final enrolment form would be sent to each participant. The forms included a list of items to bring along for the trip, a list of books to be read prior to the journey, and a synopsis of our five-point agenda. Our aim was to familiarize the participants with the overall theme of the journey before they stepped on board the train.

Preparations were in full swing. Western Railway had been extremely helpful in the allocation of coaches. We agreed to instal prefabricated shower cubicles in an empty coach to accommodate the needs of a large number of participants. A special kitchen was created, and a catering company was hired to take care of the food.

The common room, the only air-conditioned chaircar cabin, was to broadcast discussions on the train to the participants in the other coaches.

As the date of departure approached, our small two-room office in Kala Ghoda took on a life of its own. Facilitators came from various parts of the country and some from abroad. Sanjay, my brother-in-law, and Raghav, along with Colonel Suresh Patil and other organizers, were to make sure that the train was ready. Shipra, Gauri and my father-in-law were coordinating our visits to the places on our itinerary. Through TCI we had organized buses at different locations for our local commute. Given the fact that Frank had arrived from London, we also arranged for two film crews from Mumbai to accompany him.

In retrospect, it all seems incredibly difficult. Perhaps it was the sheer fun of attempting the unknown. But a promise had been made and it had to be kept.

What helped the most eventually was the energy the concept inspired amongst the organizers. In the Golden Jubilee year, we did not have to sell the project, it sold itself. What had excited us about the journey, excited other facilitators, organizers and participants as well. Our organization and fund-raising was largely independent of government aid. After our failed attempts at obtaining a student concession for the journey, we decided to minimize the help we took from the government. This gave us enormous flexibility. It allowed us not only to attract achievers, but also made the project unique. Interestingly, when we did visit government institutions, we were able to see the contrast between them and the energy and vibrancy we saw in places like Tilonia, Ralegaon Siddhi, the Bajaj auto factory and Jamshedpur. I believe that these experiences subconsciously altered the career choices of a number of participants who at the time were looking to the government as a potential employer.

As organizers, we often remarked that with such a diverse group on the train, we had no 'troublemakers'. I believe that the concept of venturing out, of sharing an adventure, thinking about the future, instinctively drew positive individuals to the journey. Those who were finally selected were optimistic in their approach to life. Their conduct on the journey reflected this attitude.

While organizing the event, we had to often fend criticism that the journey was only for the privileged. In fact, it was for young Indians who were privileged because of their intellect, dynamism, idealism and energy, and not necessarily because they had money. Almost 70 per cent of the participants were sponsored and the remaining paid a nominal fee for the journey. We also saw to it that the participants were selected from diverse backgrounds. At one point in November, when we realized that participation was skewed towards the North, we held a press conference in Chennai to drum up participation from the South.

But a more insidious criticism went to the heart of our purpose. It was said that the money spent on the *yatra* could have instead gone to the poor. This was an attitude we had battled against from the inception of the project. Most of those we spoke with, especially those from the wealthy West, wanted to focus on the poor of India. When they talked of lifting the 'masses from poverty', however, it seemed to imply a certain dependence, as if such charity was the only way the poor could be helped. This 'charity mentality' stunted local institutions. In reality – as we discovered during our travels – the glass was half-full. We had to believe in ourselves and harness our capabilities. We would welcome outside help when it was required, but not before we put our shoulders to the task. In many areas, we knew that India was self-sufficient. Our talented group, many of whom were poor, were capable of transforming their own lives and the life of the nation.

At this point in the journey, we organized the participants into seven groups in order to debate our seven-point agenda. Each group would decide a time when they had to meet, and each batch was assigned a facilitator who was to guide the discussion. Once an initial discussion was completed, the group would present its view to the remaining participants in the common room. This would form the basis of an interactive session, which then allowed the group to re-debate the topic to arrive at a conclusion. We hoped that such a process would ensure the participation of the entire train, keeping everyone involved and informed.

We arrived in Amritsar in the midst of such debates. The train had been delayed by an entire day due to fog. As our train pulled into Amritsar, a gentle rain had started to fall. We were greeted by a member of the governor's office, and our first destination was the infamous Jallianwala Bagh.

This bloodied 'garden' surrounded by walls on three sides was the scene of a massacre led by Brigadier-General Reginald Dyer who in a bizarre show of force started firing on an unarmed gathering. The year was 1919.

The rain had slowed to a drizzle. It is difficult to describe how we felt at Jallianwala Bagh. We stood in a line along the memorial thinking of those who had sacrificed their lives. We knew that the massacre had jolted the entire country into realizing the true nature of the British Raj. As we observed the pockmarks made by bullets in the walls of the Bagh, we knew that each nameless person who had fallen had not died in vain. That fateful afternoon, in the words of John Keay, '…the moral pretence of British rule had been riddled into transparency'.

When we arrived at the Golden Temple, dusk was setting in. The reflection of a lit Harmandir Sahib shimmered in the sarovar, as we did the *parikrama* around the perimeter of the temple quietly, listening to the recitation of prayers in the sanctum. The *gurbani* was mesmeric, and we walked on tiptoe, as if not wanting to disturb the serene atmosphere as thousands converged in prayer. Hardly anyone spoke.

As we were emerging from the temple, Raghav dared me to take a plunge with him in the icy cold waters of the temple pool. It was 8 p.m. at the end of December and the temperature was just above freezing. But Raghav and I have survived a number of adventures together, so we took our holy dip much to the distress of the other organizers, who felt we would definitely take ill. But we both knew that this *amrit sarovar,* which had given the city its name, could only cure.

The temple, with its sonorous chants, taught us the power of Guru Nanak's teaching – that society must treat everyone as equal. It taught us the power of humility as we watched pilgrims cleaning shoes and washing utensils in the kitchen. As we sat down to have our dinner at the *langar* where food was being served to the musical clank of steel buckets, we observed how Punjab had been reinvigorated by the teachings of Nanak.

Then began the festivities. We had been invited by a college in Amritsar to view a performance of *gidda* and *bhangra* folk dances. The strain of the first few days – the organizational debates, the emotion at the Jallianwala Bagh, the spiritual experience at the Golden Temple – suddenly found release in the colourful *bhangra* as the participants all got on stage to join in the revelry. They clambered on stage en masse to join in the *bhangra*, even though some had seen it performed for the first time that evening.

It was interesting to see the reaction of our participants from the South. They had not experienced North India, and for them this was an adventure made more real by the evening's festivity. They were experiencing the boisterous North for the first time, the warmth and liveliness that is the language of Punjab.

As the heartland of Punjab, Amritsar had been witness to a number of political ups and downs since independence. Post-partition, it led the renaissance of Punjab as the spiritual and cultural capital. Numerous dislocated Punjabis displayed enormous resilience in starting afresh and making a success of their lives through their natural entrepreneurial spirit. The Punjabis in general, and the Sikhs in particular, are known across the world for their direct approach to business and relationships.

My recollections of Punjab as a young boy studying in Sangrur were of verdant fields irrigated by overflowing canals. I still remember visiting the Bhakra dam, one of the highest straight gravity dams in the world. Huge turbine shafts were being completed and in the dull echoes of its cavernous tunnels, I could hear the drum roll of Punjab's prosperity. The militancy of the 1980s, culminating in the siege of the Akal Takht and the assassination of Indira Gandhi was a setback. Barring those dark years, the state of Punjab has demonstated a resilience and can-do spirit that are integral to its character.

By this time, the train was more than a group of strangers; individual personalities and characters were beginning to emerge. Akhtar, a blind student from Mumbai, impressed everyone with his incisive questions. Karthik, the grand-nephew of Dr Raja Ramanna – the father of the Indian nuclear weapons programme – had written an open letter to the scientist criticizing him on the nuclear test in 1974. As I differed with Karthik, this was a subject of much debate between us. Mohit, who had come from a small town called Kathgodam in Uttaranchal, was better read than the average city-dweller twice his age. And Deepa, from Bangalore, had led the women's National Cadet Corps (NCC) battalion at the Republic Day parade in Delhi. And there were many more talented participants.

At this point in the journey, the participants began to realize that learning from one another was perhaps far more important than just looking to the outside world or looking to the organizers for guidance. We had set up sleeping cabins in such a manner that there was a mix of people clubbed together. Diversity was deliberately maintained in each cabin, which made the learning process richer.

The facilitators played a key role in the journey. Their task was to coach and guide discussions around the seven-point agenda while allowing participants to explore and find solutions on their own. The facilitators provided the tools for discussion but allowed discussions to flow unhindered within these groups. Equally important were the informal discussions that were beginning to take place within the compartments.

Colonel Suresh Patil stood out amongst the organizers. He had written to us when he heard of the journey, and volunteered to be the main person in charge of the train. He ensured that everyone behaved, was on time, and in general kept discipline. After retiring from the Army, Colonel Patil had started Green Thumb, an organization that was working towards sustainable development in Pune. His presence brought a certain order to our progress which held us in good stead during the journey.

Facilitators like Raghav, Steven, Bridget, Deepali, Shefali and others worked in the corporate sector. Deepali had worked overtime prior to the journey to mobilize sponsorship in India. There were a few who were full-time social workers like Sudeshna and Amiya. Sudeshna ran a charity in Pune aptly called Sparrows which focused on taking care of street children. There was also a group of handicapped girls from an orphanage in Pune who were looked after by T. Shanti and her team.

There were four street children accompanying Sudeshna on the journey, one of whom, Shubham, stood out. He had been raised by Sudeshna. Shubham had run away from home when he was eleven. When he came to Sparrows as a runaway, Sudeshna spotted his innate talents and took him under her wing. He was so moved by this rare show of affection that he changed his name to Shubham Sudeshna. In one conversation Shubham stated simply in Hindi, 'I say that Didi has given me life.' As he was forced to work from childhood, he did not want to see anyone subjected to child labour: 'When I grow up, I will do something for these children. I will send all the children to school and will let them play a lot.' He loved football; he felt it taught him to follow rules and learn teamwork.

Rachna, a facilitator from McCann Ericsson, was conducting a media profile of young students on the train by organizing workshops. Students participated in discussions on their aspirations, their needs, and how they viewed the world. A roving journalist and photographer for *Ananda Vikatan*, a Tamil magazine, was also travelling with us, and sent his reports from the train regularly to his head office. This gave us better coverage in the South than we had received in the North. Rajesh, a radio journalist, recorded conversations in Hindi, which were later to be broadcast as a radio diary. We had been requested by Colgate, our sponsors, to send a daily report to the *Times of India*. This not only kept the country at large informed about the *yatra*, but it was also a relief to parents as they could track our progress through the reports, especially useful as mobile phones were not as ubiquitous as they are now.

Gauri chose to stay back in Mumbai to supervise the command centre of the journey. Our first child was expected in February, and her doctor had forbidden Gauri to travel with us. Her presence gave the parents visiting our office a sense of reassurance. Her energy even at that advanced stage of pregnancy was remarkable. She made sure that the reception committees at different stages of the journey were kept informed.

However, what became more and more visible to me was that the train was subtly split into two invisible groups. One group was largely from the urban areas of India, while the second, a quieter group, belonged to the smaller towns and rural areas. Among the organizers too, there was a subtle schism: those who saw the journey as an opportunity to interact and mingle with young, talented minds and share with them a new vision of India, and those who saw in the journey an unfolding of the past, a return to Gandhi's India.

Our passion for India – and the objective of the journey – stemmed from a belief that a generation has to sacrifice itself so that a country can be built and institutions can be nurtured. To help build a nation is difficult but it brings with it the joys of creation. We saw this journey as a debt we owed to our country for having given us so much.

But for a section of the participants, the journey was different. For them, India had arrived. Forcing oneself to 'build' and 'create institutions for tomorrow' was an outdated notion and reflected my 'mofussil town' upbringing. The Indian metros had everything the nation required, and it was time to enjoy what was on offer. This difference in perspective presented itself at different stages of the journey.

Another debate that exemplified the wider debate on India originated from Leoni Schebel, a German participant of Korean origins. Leoni had been sponsored by Dr Gautam Sen at the London School of Economics. She brought with her a curious combination of eastern intuition and Protestant rationalism from Germany. She took me aside one day and expressed her reservations on what she saw on the journey. Given Germany's troubled history and the role a misguided nationalism had played in it, she felt uncomfortable with the morning rendition of *Vande Mataram* and our celebration of India's fiftieth anniversary with such vigour.

The inclusion of international students in the *yatra* was a deliberate strategy. We felt that celebrating the fiftieth anniversary of an independent and democratic India should have global participation. One of the key themes we had chosen for the seven-point agenda was India and the globe. In our discussions, we saw India as an open country, willing to listen to the outside world and wanting its ideas to be heard outside. For us, this love for the nation was inclusive. For a young nation, this love could be nurtured and converted into a positive energy for nation-building. In a world that was fast shrinking through bits and bytes ,only such an appeal for nation-building could be heard, understood and appreciated. Not everyone in the *yatra* thought in this manner. For some, *Vande Mataram* was just a matter of national pride. The louder you sang it, the more patriotic you were.

For the vast majority though, it represented a step forward, it represented an India where the future was positive.

Anup, a young participant from the UK, had experienced India before, but never with the intensity this journey offered. His experience of India was based on visits to relatives in Gujarat, mostly in the company of his parents. His place of birth and residence was the UK, but he had a strange fascination for India which pulled him here. At the time, he had a set of examinations coming up but decided to take part in the first two weeks of the journey to see this different side of India.

Anup initially felt uncomfortable with the intensity of the experience. He felt like an outsider while interacting with a set of students who were often overly passionate about India. His was a rational approach, and the emotion he saw in other Indians of his age was new to him. But he later learnt from visits to Tilonia, Jaipur and Amritsar that another side to India existed, an India which perhaps even his parents did not know of. In his fellow travellers, he saw talent that surprised him. He met people like Mohit, who at a tender age had devoured all of Ayn Rand's works while based in a small town in Uttaranchal. Anup saw how a blind student, Radheyshyam, had travelled alone from Jabalpur to join us on the train in Mumbai. These participants left a lasting impression on the thirty-odd NRIs and non-Indian participants and organizers. In turn, the NRI participants ensured that our discussions were not just led by the emotion of building a nation, but had a practical flavour, backed by analysis and coherent logic.

Sumitra Golikeri, an Indian-American participant, expressed this debate within the NRI contingent by penning this poem:

Identity Crisis

Who am I? What do I see?
I have come here to discover the true me.
There I am different, here I am too,
Either way, I am left with a blurry view.

I am Amercian to some, Indian to the rest.
All seem to be putting me under some large test.
Never quite fitting into the larger scene,
Constantly shifting, ready to scream!

My accent is big in one foreign land,
My parents' is too on the other hand.
Different styles different paces,
Me trying to keep up in both the races.

I will continue to try to meld the two,
A difficult task but one I must do.

4

Delhi Durbar: A Look at the Indian Polity

Just because you don't take an interest in politics, doesn't mean politics won't take an interest in you.

– Pericles

Monday, 29 December 1997

The first concerted attempt at discussing and forming opinions on the seven-point agenda took place during the ride into Delhi. Individual groups had been formed by this time, with lessons in team work from Steven and Bridget. The teams now understood each other well. A 'life timeline' introduction technique introduced by Steven and Bridget had been an immediate success. With the help of this technique, each participant was able to share the highs and lows of his life with the rest of the group. As individuals started to open up to each other through discussions, participants drew peaks on the flip chart when they had cleared an examination or had fallen in love. Their graphs swooned on losing a dear one, or failing to make a grade. I wish I had kept some of these flip charts, for they expressed the increasing buoyancy and humour on the train.

Karthikeyan, a participant from Tiruchirapalli, Tamil Nadu, was particularly enjoying this leg of the journey. He had learnt of this project from a press conference in Chennai which had received extensive coverage in the South. Karthikeyan spoke no Hindi and had never travelled outside Tamil Nadu. We deliberately put him in a compartment with Milind and Devang and others who were not from the South. Karthikeyan's contribution to his group was to sketch a map of India, then display it on the wall of his compartment. He then traced the journey as we circled India, savouring every dot on the map like a new-found pearl. I only spoke to him a few times during the journey but his annual tricolour greeting card remained a regular Independence Day feature for several years.

Karthikeyan's positive attitude reminded me of my meetings with some of the luminaries we had met while the journey was being organized, and the different attitudes we encountered. We had written to Nani Palkhivala, the renowned jurist and economist, to accompany us on the train to talk about changes in the Constitution over the years. He was an eminent public figure, someone we looked up to as an expert on the Indian Constitution. At the time, he was the chairman of Associated Cement Company. He agreed to meet with me in Bombay House, the headquarters of the Tata group of companies. He listened to me quietly for over fifteen minutes as I described the objective of the train journey, the five-point agenda and its forward-looking objective. After a long pause, he responded, 'I like the concept of the *yatra*, I like your style, but at this juncture,

I do not see a future for the country. I am afraid I cannot take part in the journey.'

There was an uncomfortable silence as I digested his views. He was one of the nation's most respected figures, who had done so much for the country. I blurted out, 'If stalwarts like you give up, how do you expect us to inspire the young? If you are as despondent as this, what hope do we have?' In the end Nani Palkhivala did not take part in the journey but he did give us his blessings and good wishes.

I also met with S.P. Godrej, the patriarch of the Godrej family and a household name in India. I had gone to seek sponsorship for the journey. He saw me at his Vikhroli compound in Mumbai with his biographer. He was wearing a black ribbon on his sleeve as he viewed the fiftieth year of Indian independence as a failed milestone. He listened to me, agreed to sponsor two students, and was gracious and kind, but with a heavy heart. He had witnessed India's missed opportunities, and having seen his company through an enormous journey of growth, he saw an India that was far less vibrant.

The pervasive feeling appeared to be that India was stalling – politically as well as economically. There had been a series of political changes, and the country was headed towards one more general election well before the end of the five-year period when it normally was due. The extent of political fragmentation and a lack of national direction was palpable. These veterans viewed India as a static project.

In contrast, the spirit we observed on the train was one of optimism, of striving. This optimism was more than the idealism of youth. It represented an India which could dream, an India where the future was lit with the fires of hope. The younger generation was ready to take on 'Project India' with its own positive frame of reference. Our call for a generation sacrificing itself so that future generations could have a better life, struck an immediate chord with many of these participants. In many ways, this was similar to what Nani Palkhivala had done all his life, but there is an energy and buoyancy that has flowered in the national mainstream since then.

In the nine years since the journey, India has found its place on the international map. The younger generation has largely been responsible for this resurgent India. It is due to their hard work, dedication and commitment that the service industries have a leading position on the international stage. But India's success has been as much a private victory as a public one. The younger generation's approach to life is clearly different from that of the previous generation of public figures. This generation is ambitious and willing to work hard for personal fulfilment. In the process, it has taken India forward as well. Perhaps our senior leaders were disheartened by this materialistic approach. Perhaps it was simply their frame of reference which I believe led to a false sense of despondency.

We believed that accumulating personal wealth through integrity, hard work and excellence was central to a country's growth. These values distinguish growth from greed and are the foundations of a lasting nation. In Indian philosophy, *artha* and *kama* sit alongside *dharma* and *moksha*. The ancient scriptures seem quite modern in this respect: they speak of the pursuit of wealth as a legitimate human aspiration, but through right means, and without losing sight of the larger goal of life. Freedom to secure and enjoy material wealth can only come from the bonds of ethical discipline.

~

From Amritsar, on the way to Delhi, the common room became our busiest place of work. The groups at this point had completed their first discussion on the seven-point agenda, which was followed by a question-and-answer session. The *azad gaon* and *azad nagar* groups were particularly active. Inspired by a model village in Tilonia, and with the advanatage of having a few engineers amongst them, they were coming up with creative ideas to strengthen the Indian infrastructure ten to twenty years hence. Other groups also presented their ideas in the common room after having first discussed them amongst themselves.

From the very beginning, we challenged the participants to think in the 'future tense', to focus on India's future. Our brief to the participants was to think not only of what they wanted to build, but how they would go about it, including marshalling the resources to implement their mission. In that sense, the thinking process was based on action. Building a nation required the implementation of a vision, not mere theorizing.

As organizers, we left the participants free to draw their own conclusions. Our central theme was excellence. We wanted participants to be exposed to India and the people – some of them exceptional – whom they met, but in the end we wanted them to be inspired to seek excellence in their own way. We did not want them to go away thinking that everyone could or should become a Bunker or an Aruna Roy. Our view was that 'Project India' was best served by excelling in one's chosen field. This could mean starting a company, working in the corporate sector, in the government, or working with an NGO. Excellence fuelled innovation; 'building India' required change and creativity. These themes of excellence and change guided us to structure our journey to visit places like Tilonia. Our search was for individuals and institutions who had silently persevered to bring about change. Munshi Premchand, the famous writer, echoes our thoughts in the phrase *'neev ki eent'* – the brick that holds our foundation together.

As we were working together in groups, we also observed that our participants were a microcosm of the real India. As they travelled through unfamiliar surroundings, meeting with visionaries, they were more open and forthcoming. In this mix of people, we also saw the many divisions we suffered within.

For the first few days of the journey, the English-speaking section of the train was ebullient and loquacious. However, during various discussions and debates, it became clear that there was an equally strong contingent from the so-called 'non-metro' areas. This group was not as fluent in English, did not have the same mindset as the others, but in my view, they thought more deeply about India. As they were less anglicized, they seemed more intuitive and grounded while addressing developmental issues, rather than aligning themselves with what was being read in the English press. Their approach seemed surer, although they lagged behind in their ability to express themselves. Having grown up in a small town myself, I was familiar with this side of India; an India that perhaps spoke broken English but was as knowledgeable as its urban counterpart.

Karthik Rammana put it thus: People Like Them (PLTs), were from small-town India; and People Like Us (PLUs), were people who belonged to the bigger cities. The PLUs led the discussions in the first week. They were the questioning majority during the sessions held in the common room, but when it came down to the nitty-gritty of developmental issues, they were not always the first to contribute. The passion, intuition and knowledge of the small-town PLTs was becoming more apparent.

India still lives largely in rural areas and smaller towns. Only a fraction of India – by some estimates only 5 per cent – speaks fluent English. That does not prevent India from being the third largest English-speaking country in the world after the UK. In employment terms, of the 400 million people in the workforce today, only 7 per cent are in the organized sector of the economy, to which the PLUs will naturally gravitate. By 2025, it is expected that more than 60 per cent of Indians – over 800 million – will still continue to live in rural areas.

Which of these groups will lead India in the future? Probably both in their own ways. The PLUs have their eyes on universities in the USA and UK. They will no doubt succeed, but by skimming the surface of India. The second group from the smaller towns has grown up around vernacular literature, and understands the reality of mofussil India. Clearly, there is no clear division between the two. The beauty of our journey was that both PLUs and PLTs were beginning to understand each other's perspective. Karthik from Mumbai was now working closely with Karthikeyan from Tiruchirapalli. While their differences complemented each other, it was instructive to see that despite their meagre knowledge of English, the PLTs were now emerging to stand on par with the other participants.

From Amritsar, our train was due to visit Agra, where a visit to the Taj Mahal had been organized. However, we discovered that the Agra visit would cost us an additional day, and a decision was taken to go to Agra by bus. On our visit to the Taj Mahal, a controversy regarding an oil refinery and its effect on the monument instigated a debate on sustainable development. It was believed that unless careful precautions were taken, pollutants from the refinery could mar this wonder of the world. The environment and sustainable development group was particularly perturbed and the issue made for an interesting discussion on the ride back from Agra.

Raghav volunteered to lead the bus ride to Agra before he got off at Delhi to return to Australia. His contribution to the journey was seminal. He had acted as a personal companion and counsel to me; I was able to share my deepest concerns and joys with him. As a natural leader, he had established a fluid bond with the participants. In that crucial first week, without his contribution, the journey would have been very difficult for me. As we parted company at Safdarjang railway station in Delhi, Frank volunteered to capture on camera what was a life-long bear hug between us. Another week of companionship was added to our many adventures together, one I will remember and be grateful for ever.

Wednesday, 31 December 1997

The Delhi we were visiting was a modern metropolis, second only to Mumbai in population, and far ahead of any other city of India in terms of vehicular population. In addition to the city itself, towns like Noida and Gurgaon near it were virtual extensions of the capital city. But the seven cities that remain buried below the surface of modern Delhi are not forgotten. Their reminders are everywhere, in the hundreds of monuments spread all across the city, and in the forts whose proud ramparts still dominate the landscape.

There was so much to do in Delhi that we were spoilt for choice. We decided to spend some time in the Rashtrapati Bhavan where we were welcomed and taken around the enormous building by the Bhavan staff. The president himself was on a state visit, but his enormous residence told us its own story. It is said that the

Rashtrapati Bhavan is about the size of two Buckingham Palaces and five White Houses. As we walked through the plush red-carpeted Durbar Hall, our hosts described how the soft carpet had been specifically sprung to help with ball dancing in the Viceroy's Ballroom. While this grandeur and size impressed us, the main debate within its vast halls and gardens was on politics. After all, it is here, in this great city of durbars and politics, that an emergent India was being shaped.

We discussed the Indian Constitution which had been formed in the adjoining Parliament House some forty-seven years ago. Was it flexible enough to be moulded to the circumstances of today? Were key principles in the Constitution like the Directive Principles of State Policy still relevant? These principles asked the state to guarantee welfare and employment to every citizen, which was not only unachievable but weakened the rest of the constitutional document. After the liberalization of the Indian economy and the demise of the old socialist thinking, was it necessary to restructure the Constitution to give impetus to growth and nation-building?

Our Constituent Assembly, while framing the final constitutional draft in November 1949, invoked the words of Thomas Jefferson: 'The idea that institutions established for the use of the nation cannot be touched nor modified, even to make them answer their end... is most absurd and against the nation itself. Yet our lawyers and priests generally inculcate this doctrine, and suppose that preceding generations held the earth more freely than we do...'

We also reflected on the 'DNA of a nation builder'. The nation-building process required an approach qualitatively different from that which gave us independence. Our founding fathers were largely lawyers with a preference to discuss and adjudicate within a given legal, economic and social framework. They turned their skills successfully towards making the British leave India. In the years after independence they put their energies into consolidating this hard-won freedom and putting systems in place for governance. But now, perhaps, what is required is a little more flexibility, an ability to rise above the system, so to speak. A framework which allows us to step outside our comfort zones, create enterprises, both social and economic and build new institutions – a process that requires mavericks.

But the present system in India loathes mavericks. Anyone who wants to change the system will threaten the rent the 'durbar' seeks from its citizens. While individuals within this system are talented, the purpose of the system is to maintain control and a status quo. It resists any impetus to change. It hinders innovation and enterprise.

Our administrative system was designed in the times of the Raj when Delhi was primarily concerned with ruling and controlling its far-flung empire. It was designed to be a 'benign dictatorship'.

Our group recognized that at the time of independence while the new Constitution brought freedom, Indians remained dependent on the state in a manner similar to the days of the Raj. As the viceroy and British administrators moved out of Luytens' Delhi, it was taken over by another type of durbar which had been seeded by the Raj. The same physical structures, the same ochre walls of these bungalows and buildings kept the ideas of the empire alive. Our politicians, who were accountable to the public, remained tentative in reforming the administrative system, and the country has suffered as a result.

The durbar culture was further strengthened by the economic controls that limited growth for many decades. First instituted in Nehru's time, under Indira Gandhi they became stifling until the process of opening up the economy was taken up in 1991.The battle for liberalization is by no means over. A strong lobby continues to argue for retaining more control over the economy and a stronger role for the public sector.

We felt that there were further divisions within the bureaucracy. Senior, talented officers in the national services are underpaid and overworked in comparison to people working in the private sector, and are naturally more pliable than the upright Indian Civil Service officer of yesteryear. This layer of management oversees a mass of overpaid government workers who, we felt, deny service to the common man. In recent years, this layer of management is feeling threatened like never before by change and privatization.

But the burden of the bureaucratic system is even greater at a psychological level. It is a story of limiting talent and idealism. Upright, idealistic and talented individuals in the first few years in the civil service try to change the system. But the system is resistant to change. It was designed to control. And this mode of functioning did not change after we gained independence. Even George Curzon, Viceroy of India, one of the architects of this system of government, ridiculed the administrative procedures in 1901: 'Round and round like the diurnal revolution of the earth went the file, stately, solemn, sure and slow, and now in due season it had completed its orbit, and I am invited to register the concluding stage.'

In the middle of this discussion, I realized that I had to make a phone call to a journalist who had promised to cover the journey in Delhi. Mobile phones had just started becoming popular in India. At the time, Max Touch (now Hutch) had given us five precious mobile phones as part of the overall sponsorship package. On the lawns of the Rashtrapati Bhavan, I handed my mobile phone to Mohit, and asked him to speak to the journalist. Mohit still remembers how he looked in wonderment at this small gadget thrust into his hands. He punched in the large number of digits that I had given him in some confusion. He was used to five-digit telephone numbers. He then waited to hear the phone ring. When nothing happened, he turned to another *yatri* in panic to find that he had to press the green button for the call to go through. It was with a sense of wonder that he then spoke on a wireless device, standing in the midst of a 50-foot lawn. It was our first taste of the technological change that was beginning to take place in India. Little did we know that within a few years mobile phones would by far outstrip the number of landlines in the country.

Change, we discussed, must come from a responsive administration. These representatives have to be accountable to the local population, held directly responsible or rewarded in the next election by the people, not by a coterie of middlemen or a group of detached administrators. The Panchayati Raj system has started this process. The iron framework of a central administration with senior and talented leadership must remain, but a wholesale re-examination of the way modern India is administered is required. A number of commentators in the national and international media talk of the economic unshackling of the country in 1991. What is less advertised is the Panchayati Raj system and its impact on ground level development and the political life of the nation. One only wishes this had happened earlier in our national journey.

On the lawns of the Rashtrapati Bhavan, we also debated on the need for a more stable political system, one that could override the uncertainties of coalition governments that were being formed by diverse parties coming together, only to break up after a few months when they were unable to get along with each other. Could the prime minister really do much with a cabinet that represented such a multiplicity of views, and small parties that were more interested in the spoils of power than anything else? Did we require a stronger system of government? Was the Westminster model adequate for governing a nation of more than a billion people?

Against this political backdrop we discussed a social question – the need for affirmative action. In a society as stratified as that of India, where underprivileged sectors still exist in abject poverty, affirmative action is required. But should that not be confined to spreading education? India has to create the most significant affirmative action programme on the planet, but its approach should centre around providing the underprivileged with education and skills to enable them to fend for themselves. Such an approach allows talent to prosper and adds value to the human resource talent pool of the nation. The money spent will not only genuinely help the underprivileged, it will also maintain national competitiveness. Clearly, this strategy has been ignored by the government.

We felt that India's rationale had to be dramatically different. Our view was that the state would have to regulate more, do less. The state had to be a coach rather than a demanding captain. It would then over time earn the respect of its people.

We had organized a debate in the evening at IIT Delhi, my alma mater. Participants and organizers spent New Year's Eve in the seminar hall with four notable figures of Indian public life – Dr Kiran Bedi, Mark Tully, Dr Rajendra Pachauri and Dr V. S. Raju, Director of IIT Delhi.

I had first met Kiran Bedi during my travels in the North-East with Shipra, her daughter Reva, and Gauri. We had visited places like Dimapur and Kohima in Nagaland, Imphal in Manipur, and Aizawl in Mizoram. Our journey drew an arc next to the Burmese border. It opened up our mind to a region tucked away from the national consciousness. Kiran, at that time, was posted in Aizawl. She was known across the country as a fearless and outspoken police officer even then. She demonstrated her mettle as a tough policewoman in bringing some order to Delhi's notoriously undisciplined traffic, and later while in charge of the high-security Tihar Jail, helped improve conditions and change the lives of the inmates by a series of measures, including yoga courses. We were in Aizawl, when I happened to chance upon her name as the superintendent of police in the local directory. We requested a meeting. In a location that was closer to Bangkok than to Delhi, visitors were welcome.

Our brief meeting in her bungalow turned into a two-hour dialogue. When we wrote to her about the journey, she was immediately responsive, and we agreed that the best way forward was for her to speak at the seminar at IIT Delhi. Kiran went on to be awarded the Ramon Magsaysay Award for her path-breaking work at Tihar, among other things.

Mark Tully was similarly intrigued by the journey. He wanted to interact with young minds, and although we had written to him relatively late in the day, he agreed to join us on New Year's Eve. Mark is a true India-lover, and we found his insights into India often deeper than those of most Indians. He has the power of being both an outsider and an insider, with over thirty-five years of reporting experience in India. We had grown up with his voice on the BBC; it was synonymous with 'the real truth'.

Dr Rajendra Pachauri was a family friend who had done seminal work in environmental development and sustainability. At that time, he was the director of the Tata Energy Research Institute (TERI) and had put TERI firmly on the environmental policy map of India.

We had met with Dr V.S. Raju, the Director of IIT Delhi, when we were still organizing the *yatra.* He gave us a patient hearing, and was convinced that as an alumnus, I was doing the right thing. Initially unsure about the feasibility of the journey, he agreed to host a seminar and gave his insights on modern Indian education and the growing area of technical education.

By this time, the fatigue of working non-stop for the past four months, the first difficult and emotional leg of the journey, and the bone-chilling cold of Delhi were catching up. I felt tired and needed a day's rest, but knew that I could not afford this luxury. The other participants and facilitators were also tired, but were looking forward to the debates at IIT Delhi.

We started the evening by screening the video *Maa Tujhe Salam*, loaned to us by Bala Bharat and Kanika Meyer. Bala and Kanika had left lucrative careers in the advertising industry to set up a media company that focused on India-centric themes. They had first come across our promotional poster in an Indian bookshop in London. When we approached them to accompany us on the journey, they were touring the world interviewing eminent personalities as a way of showcasing India in its fiftieth year of independence. They immediately grasped the importance of the journey and loaned us the A.R. Rahman video and we tried to screen it at most of the events we organized. Against a soundtrack of Rahman's *Vande Mataram*, the video contained inspiring shots of India, ranging from the panoramic deserts of Rajasthan we had recently crossed, to the frosty heights of Ladakh. The deep blue seas that lapped the coast were contrasted with the green forests of the country. But against these physical manifestations of India was a cultural theme. Young children running with the tricolour flag in a small village of Rajasthan; an army of bare-backed villagers hosting a giant flag in a desert; a young dancer under the fronds of a forest in the Himalayas. This short video, screened across the country, managed to encapsulate the visual feast that unfolded as we travelled its length and breadth.

The idea behind the seminar at IIT Delhi was to take an original approach to the issues that India faced. We felt that material progress had to be embraced within India's own social, environmental and economic framework. This required us to take ideas from elsewhere, but adapt to our reality and needs.

The discussion that followed the screening of the video was a study in contrasts. Kiran was the dynamic *devi*, passionate in every point she made. She emphasized that self-improvement was the first and most important step in building a healthy nation.

Mark was a study in cautious optimism. On the one hand, he was positive about the general direction India was taking, but on the other, he was cautious about our burgeoning bureaucracy. He warned, 'Even fifty years after independence the British colonial system continues to dominate our bureaucracy.'

Dr Pachauri, as the director of TERI, talked about looking at India's economic growth with an eye on sustainability. He reinforced our belief that blindly following industrialized countries was sub-optimal. In our race towards development, it was crucial to understand the underlying environmental impact, and to ensure that human parameters in a billion-strong India were understood. He said, 'In terms of sustainable development, we must meet the needs of the present without sacrificing the needs of the future.'

Dr V. S. Raju, as an eminent educationist, applauded what he saw as an important 'out of class learning', and agreed to support future *yatras* in and around the IIT curriculum which led us to coin the phrase 'semester on wheels'.

During the seminar, participants chipped in. Poonam, from Chennai, was vocal in her views on women's issues, and we put her next to the main speakers on stage. Colonel Patil, who had done excellent ground-level work on the environment through his Green Thumb organization in Pune, also led and contributed to discussions on the environment and sustainable development.

I had asked my guru and teacher from IIT Delhi, Dr P.L. Dhar, to speak to the participants on Vipassana meditation. Dr Dhar was a frugal individual who, while a technologist by training, ensured that his personal style reflected his belief in a simple life. He had been part of a group that introduced Vipassana meditation to IIT Delhi. Vipassana as a meditation technique taught students to control their minds through observance of silence and a strict dietary regime. I remember that when the course was first introduced at the adjoining Aravali hostel, a small number of participants elected to leave after a day or two of silence. It was too much for them. Those who stayed on, though, emerged with calm written on their faces. Today Dr Dhar spoke of that meditation, its powers to still the mind, and how people benefited in being able to control their senses and lead a more complete life.

Dr Dhar had taught me mechanical engineering, but he also took a course which was one of the more over-subscribed humanities electives at IIT Delhi – Science and Humanism. In this course, he challenged us to think originally. The course sought to combine the intuition of the East with the scientific vocabulary of the West. But more importantly, it challenged us to think in terms relevant to India, and to not merely ape USA or Europe. For instance, one of the projects he was involved with was conversion of the heat energy of the hot water springs in Almora into a refrigeration system for cooling medicines which had to be stored at low temperatures. Electricity was not available in the hills of Almora, and his solution was to use a natural resource with the help of technology relevant to local conditions.

'Science and Humanism' appealed to us on another level. Most entrants to IIT are familiar with modern physics. The course included reading *The Tao of Physics.* In this remarkable book, Fritjof Capra, a Swedish physicist and systems theorist, links ancient concepts from the East to modern physics. The synthesized and holistic view of the East arrived at a similar truth to that unveiled by the atomic accelerators of the European Organization for Nuclear Research (CERN). Sub-atomic oscillations in the cyclotron in Berkeley were reflections of the cosmic dance of Shiva. The Sufi poetry of Chishti at a deeper level could interpret a reality similar to that comprehended by Einstein as he cycled to his office in Berne. For technologists, it offered a bridge to link Indian philosophy with the scientific endeavours we were about to embark on. During our course, we also got an early hint that the Newtonian world-view of the industrial West was beginning to be challenged. In this new world, India may have something original to offer.

While the IITs have been applauded for their excellence in technological training, a less well-documented contribution is the 'democratic experience' it offers to students. Entrance to the institute is strictly by merit. During my time, merit and talent came from different parts of India. It came in the form of Raghav, from Motilal School of Sports in Haryana; it came in the form of Jhaji from Bihar, who never missed an opportunity to take a potshot at the metro convent crowd; it came in the form of Arvind, the silent intellectual, and Arun, who brought a different kind of integrity to the group. Dr Dhar's attempts to make us original in our thinking found fertile ground amongst this diverse group.

Our seminar ended with a screening of a short audio-visual on the life of an ordinary IIT Delhi student. Veenu Pasricha, my classmate, had created this audio-visual at the end of our four-year term, and it had become part of the induction process for new students at the institute at the beginning of every year. As Veenu screened it to the participants that evening, a much younger Raghav appeared on screen. He had left for Australia earlier that day, so participants were surprised to see him re-appear as the protagonist in the film. Veenu's camera captured the daily life of a young Raghav as he brushed his teeth, hurried to classes – a scene rare in real life! – and took part in hostel water fights. While the music of Pink Floyd and The Who played in the background, he was seen enjoying the pleasures of the outdoor canteen run by Kishanlal. Chikadoo, the favoured waiter, sounded like a metronome as he kept the canteen going. For me, it brought back warm memories from my years at IIT which were unquestionably some of the best years of my life: the pre-dawn cycle rides to the freezing computer centre where our mainframe computer evolved from punched cards to printouts; the hyperbolic-paraboloid rooftop of the convocation hall, a setting for many philosophical debates around Jiddu Krishnamurti; the late night twists and turns of elections for the BSA, BSP and other student bodies; the forbidden midnight dips in the swimming pool and, of course, the rambunctious gaiety of Rendezvous, our annual cultural festival. During our hostel social events, scruffy IITians for once took time to spruce up for their far-too-brief encounter with the girls from Delhi University.

But our years at IIT had also afforded us glimpses of history – too many of which were tragic. As a person aspiring to get into the IIT, I had returned from my wanderings in Corbett National Park on my way through Delhi to be with my parents in Jaipur. I watched a small airplane doing gravity-defying stunts over Chanakyapuri in Delhi. I was somewhat intrigued by this buzz and clatter above me, but I heard on reaching Jaipur later that day that Sanjay Gandhi had crashed his single-seater plane in Delhi. During our second year at IIT, we heard of Indira Gandhi's assassination when summons came from the nearby All India Institute of Medical Sciences (AIIMS) for her rare blood group. Later, along with my friends, I undertook a dangerous cycle-ride during curfew to attend her cremation on the banks of the Yamuna with helicopters above creating dust swirls as Rajiv Gandhi lit her funeral pyre. Long nights followed, patrolling the portals of our campus to ensure rioters did not enter. On a more positive note, the Asian Games transformed Delhi into a city of flyovers in 1984. Around the same time, the Centre for Development of Telematics (C-DoT) ushered in a telecom revolution by connecting rural India to the rest of the world. Remote villages were soon festooned with the yellow signboards of telephone booths. When so much can take place in a span of four impressionable years, one wonders if other cities and regions of India can begin to comprehend the mind of this city.

We returned to the train where Kiran Bedi agreed to join us on New Year's Eve. Veenu's father, Avinash Pasricha, who had been the photo editor of *Span* magazine, also joined us as our resident photographer from thereon. Miraculously, the catering staff had turned the empty Safdarjang railway platform into a food lounge. A campfire was assembled and Kiran swapped stories with participants over warm cups of *chai*. Kiran's presence was an inspiration for the women participants. We left Delhi in the early hours of the new year for Lucknow, a city that has shaped politics in India as no other.

5

An Evening in Lucknow: The North Energized

'Is the glass half empty or half full? Depends whether you are pouring or drinking.'

– Bill Cosby

Thursday, 1 January 1998

The fog of the North Indian winter was catching up with us. As the train crossed the Yamuna and made its way towards Lucknow, we retraced a major political artery of India. It was this route that the freedom fighters of 1857 had taken. This was also the *Dilli Chalo* route proposed by Subhash Chandra Bose during the freedom struggle. Our train, which set off from Delhi shortly after midnight, arrived in Lucknow at 4 p.m. the next day. We kept ourselves busy with discussions and debates in the common room; they took on a rhythm of their own with participants having bonded in the first week of the train journey.

Milind Singh, a young student from Mumbai, decided to join us despite an examination which required him to return to Mumbai in the third week of the journey. His parents were originally from Uttar Pradesh, although he had spent most of his student life in Mumbai. Milind was curious about the journey but also, as a natural sceptic, he was unsure how the debates would unfold. He was a wanderer at heart and he understood that this journey held the promise of adventure. Much after the lights were turned off in the compartments, his group members would continue their debates till the early hours of the morning.

A number of rituals became part of our everyday routine. We had made it a practice to play A.R. Rahman's version of *Vande Mataram* every morning. This became our theme song during the journey. Early, every morning, Colonel Patil would play the tape on the internal speaker system which was connected to all the compartments. This is the one ritual most participants still remember waking up to years after the event. Barely had we rubbed the sleep from our eyes, and we were woken up by this elevating music; the catering staff would come hurtling through the corridors with our morning tea. After the morning 'musical awakening' ritual was the bath, where the participants took turns to shower in our specially constructed shower cubicles. The serving of meals also became another ritual. The catering staff would serve breakfast and dinner with rhythmic efficiency. Packed lunches would be handed out shortly after breakfast. The caterers organized the food to reflect the cuisine of the states we were visiting. *Dhokla* in Gujarat gave way to *tandoori* cuisine in Punjab. The *misti doi* in Bengal was a precursor to the steaming *sambar* in the South. Milind and other participants had to also find time to take part in the discussions within the groups as well. Our participants were kept busy with these discussions as our train chugged slowly towards Lucknow.

We reached Lucknow, delayed by over six hours. Our hosts from King George Medical College (KGMC) were waiting to greet us with the mayor of the city, S.C. Rai. KGMC is one of the pre-eminent medical institutions of the country and our visit was led and coordinated by Dr I.D. Sharma, head of the department of Oncology. He is a member of my family and was a great supporter of the *yatra*.

On the way to KGMC, we visited the Bara Imambara. This extraordinary structure, built by Nawab Asaf-ud-Daula in the late eighteenth century, contains one of the world's largest columnless halls, with a roof that consists of interlocking bricks without the use of beams. Dusk was setting in. As the sun set, the Bara Imambara was silhouetted against the crimson sky, offering us a view that was matched only by that of the Golden Temple.

As we entered the auditorium at the KGMC, a pleasant-looking man in a Nehru jacket approached us. To my surprise, he turned out to be Edward, my friend from London, who was visiting his parents-in-law in India. His wife Rashmi and he had contributed to shaping our first thoughts on the *yatra.* We greeted each other in mock surprise as 'Dr Livingstone, I presume'. Rashmi had decided to make India her base. She lived in India, away from her children who visited her occasionally, and worked on various community development programmes around Jaipur. Individuals like Rashmi,with their unbending spirit, have done more for the country than the biggest government grant can possibly achieve.

The seminar at KGMC focused on the latest developments in medicine, their relevance to India and the ongoing debate on sustainable development. The doctors spoke at length on recent developments in hygiene, health and the emerging concern with AIDS in India.

The Urdu poetry recital that evening by one of the doctors was an instant hit. It brought out the culture and refinement of Lucknow, transporting us instantly into another world of grace and charm.

But this land has also been the centre of Indian politics since independence. As we made our way back to the train, after an outstanding repast, our thoughts turned to Uttar Pradesh. Lucknow happens to be where I spent my most formative years, imbibing its *tehzeeb* – etiquette and manner – while studying at Colvin College where I completed four years of my senior school. Here was the Gomti river where, by imitating Huckleberry Finn, we had designed a raft with the intent of floating down the river. The Bhul Bhulaiya, an ancient monument in Lucknow, intrigued us as children. Once you got inside this maze, in the 20-feet wide walls of the Bara Imambara, only an expert, and a guide rope would ensure that you found your way out. Our morning jogs in the salubrious botanical gardens still brings back fond memories, as does the main bazaar in Hazratganj.

However, the Lucknow I grew up in and the Lucknow we were visiting was, sadly, not the same. Milind, originally from U.P., was equally keen to understand the developmental paradigm of his home state. The U.P. we grew up in was confident, nuanced and progressive. Its institutions of higher learning like Allahabad University, Aligarh Muslim University, Lucknow University and Benaras Hindu University were known for their academic excellence. Its political culture was self-assured as national leaders often came from this part of India. But the Lucknow we were visiting was different. It seemed to have lost the integrity we had known as children. As the world and most of India accelerated by taking to enterprise, U.P. remained mired in politics. It lagged behind, bereft of the balancing influence of economic thinking to compensate for its political culture.

In demographic terms, U.P. is the biggest state in India with a population of 166 million, that is growing by 3 million every year. U.P. by itself ranks as the sixth-most populated area in the world, ahead of Pakistan, and just behind Brazil. It is here that the Gangetic civilization flourished. In the Vedic period, the Aryans inhabited Uttar Pradesh which they named *Madhya Desha* or Midland. In medieval times U.P. was the centre of the Mughal empire. During this period art, architecture, music and culture flourished, and remain an integral part of India's heritage.This fertile soil that is rich in history gave birth to some of the oldest cities in India. Varanasi, for instance, is probably one of the oldest cities in the world with a continuous history from the sixth century BC.

The state had considerable political power post- independence. Approximately one in every seven MPs in Parliament is from this state. Economically, however, the state has lagged. And in comparison with other states, the contrast is starker still.

Unfortunately, its political leadership finds itself unable to shake off a feudal mindset and an all-pervasive bureaucracy. During our travels, we visited Gujarat, where the bureaucracy works alongside the citizen. In contrast, in states like U.P., the government considers itself as the only instrument for effecting development and change, emasculating private institutions. As it is still the *sarkar*, a static polity and society are taking root. Instead of people coming together to effect change by organizing themselves, cleaning up their own roads, creating their own institutions, citizens have been taught to rely on the regal figure of the district administration to lead them.

Jean Dreze and Amartya Sen, renowned economists, in the book *India: Economic Development and Social Opportunity* have pointed out that in matters of social engagement, grassroot involvement is lacking in U.P. 'It's quite possible for a village school to be non-functional for as long as ten years due to teacher absenteeism and shirking without any action being taken and any collective protest being organized.'

In recent times, the situation has reached a nadir. A time for radical change may have come. For if this state declines, so will the heart of India. I do not say this out of a sense of affinity to the state, or a fond memory that others from U.P. share with me, but because of U.P.'s contribution to the country in human and cultural terms. U.P. may be land-locked, it may have a history that often keeps it boxed, but it has the potential and the character to help it break loose from its current problems and prosper once again.

We identified two hurdles that come in the way of change. The first, and most pernicious, is the lack of an entrepreneurial culture: a culture that takes pride in risk-taking, a culture that is able to create rather than administer. In a state that is dependent on the administration, creating entrepreneurial role models is the biggest challenge. Secondly, new businesses are given very little freedom to operate. While banks and micro-finance institutions are spreading across the rest of the country, their presence and impact in U.P. is still nominal in the absence of an environment that is conducive to enterprise. When a person starts a business, the bureaucratic friction in setting it up, in keeping functionaries of the system satisfied, imposes its own strains. Furthermore, infrastructure – whether it be electricity, roads, transportation or an effective and expeditious legal system – are also lacking in U.P.

While visiting Lucknow, a colleague of my father-in-law recounted how he had to close down his business of over twenty years in sheer frustration. The municipal commissioner interfered so much in the day-to-day approval of licences that in the end he thought it better to close down and sell the premises rather than battle the system. He was a well-educated, enterprising man, yet the system would not let him function.

Creating a spirit of enterprise will take time and effort, but it can be done. We also need to protect entrepreneurs from the system. If a few are able to grow and flourish, they will start rotating the flywheel of entrepreneurship by becoming role models. Agro-based industries and businesses have to be promoted on a massive scale to uplift the rural economy. We may have to provide a system of insurance for these fledgling entrepreneurs. Vocational training in IT and other knowledge-based industries also have to be given a fillip. A significant portion of the state budget has to be spent on human resource development. It has to be spent to create a skilled workforce that can lead agro-based and knowledge-based enterprises in the future. Despite the fact that the state is predominantly agrarian – 44.4 per cent are farmer households – agriculture in U.P. is far from flourishing. Twenty-seven per cent of the farmers do not like farming and feel it is unprofitable.

I have often discussed an agro-based economy with Raju Shete, a friend and entrepreneur who is trying to revolutionize food distribution across India. Raju and Hemal, his wife, were hugely supportive of the *yatra*. Their simple lives and grounded thinking have led to the creation of a business which has attracted the attention of one of the world's biggest private equity funds. His company can engender prosperity at the grassroots by seeding agro-based businesses.

Individual success stories are already emerging. Young Sajjan from a village in Deoria started a construction business by borrowing 500 rupees from a family member. He started off as a small-time contractor. Over a period of time, he borrowed 5000 rupees, and through hard work, he managed to return the money in time. He then went for a bigger loan from a local bank to get a contract for building a petrol station. The bank official noticed that Sajjan was a man of integrity. Firstly, Sajjan left his ego at home when he set out to do business, and secondly, he worked hard and with honesty. Not only did he please his customers, he also made sure that his creditors were paid in time. His contracting volume has now expanded to a crore and ten lakh, and in this time, he has built several petrol stations, some in places as far-flung as Jhansi and Gwalior. In the early days of setting up his business, he would make an early start on freezing winter mornings on his motorcycle. In the absence of proper woollens, he would use layers of old newspapers and stuff them below his shirt to ward off the cold. Today, he travels in a Toyota, still humble and unassuming. At the age of thirty-five, he has made enough money not only to secure himself a livelihood but provide employment to forty-five others.

Back on the train, we also discussed how in matters of entrepreneurship, women have consistently taken the lead. The Grameen Bank of Mohammad Yunus and SEWA, started by Ila Bhatt, are practical examples of successful entrepreneurial models where women have made a success of themselves. Women have taken the lead in matters of planning for the future, juggling different tasks at the same time and fulfilling commitments. On this basis, our analysis found U.P. severely wanting.

According to Tim Dyson, Robert Cassen and Leela Visaria in the book *Twenty First Century India: Population, Economy, Human Development and the Environment*, 'When it comes to female subordination, Uttar Pradesh, it is said, is not just backward by international and Indian standards, but is virtually in a league of its own. In every dimension of female development, health, fertility, education or employment U.P. ranks lowest or amongst the lowest in India. Its women are, obviously with exceptions, essentially confined to domestic life and subject to male domination.' In this matter, U.P. should be ideally be able to emulate the success of Maharashtra, where under the bold vision of Dr D.K. Karve the drive for women's emancipation has seen enormous success over the past decades.

The proactive support of grassroot enterprise by other states is proving to be the biggest motivator for U.P. Instead of being content with its status as a political giant, competition from smaller states is causing U.P. to re-examine itself. In an era where investments and flow of talent move towards states that create the right environment for enterprise, U.P. is slowly beginning to change. However, this is a long process and requires commitment for the long haul. It is for the younger generation to take matters in their hands and to persevere until results are visible.

We also discussed the role of Hindi and Urdu, two of the major languages spoken in U.P. These languages have spawned a literature that forms the heart of the North Indian culture. But the role of English is also important. It should not be seen as a corruptor of local culture – an argument often given by those who resist change. English should be seen as a language that can connect U.P. with the outside world.

~

It is not as if the entrepreneurial spirit is missing in U.P. Even in our family, with its large quota of public servants and bureaucrats, we have our very own entrepreneurs.

Our family is known for being animal lovers. My great-grandfather judged men by their understanding of horses. My uncle would gloat at the sight of a good pair of bullocks for our farm. So, it was no surprise that one day, led by my grandfather, twenty members of my family travelled to Sonepur to buy an elephant.

Buying an elephant is a combination of several things at once: a family picnic, a camping expedition, and a cultural exercise topped with serious negotiation. Sonepur is on the picturesque banks of the Badi Gandak river. This also happens to be the venue for the largest animal fair in Asia.

As we arrived from Gorakhpur on a train, we got down at a railway platform that at the time was famous for being the longest in the world. The noisy platform was an apt prelude to the scenes that greeted us as we entered the Sonepur fairground. A huge tented city had sprung up. Tents in thousands were neatly cut in half by a layer of smoke that persistently hung six feet above ground in winter evenings, as fireside cooks rustled up tempting dishes. This was one location where cow dung for the camp fires was not in short supply.

The morning set the stage for the 'deal'. A bewildering range of poultry, livestock and animals was on display – fowl, goats, cows, bullocks, horses, mules, monkeys and in the good old days even tigers. Elephants in hundreds stood swaying under trees, tied to their *khoonti*. The most fascinating were tuskers, some known for their 'gore record'. The larger the number of mahouts looking after a tusker, the more notorious the elephant was, and to us kids, more exciting. We then espied lovely Laxmi, a ten-year-old, standing 10-feet tall. And the family instantly fell in love.

Negotiations were about getting the price right, no matter how much we liked Laxmi. This is when we split into two teams. An advance party with Pradumna Uncle in the lead moved in. His tactic was to point out flaws in what seemed a perfectly beautiful animal. The trunk was a tad too long, the spine wavered a bit, the tail swooshed the ground. My cousin, as a newly educated expert side-kick, started pointing to a flaw in the foot. At this point, the seller seemed a bit shaken. Once this tactic was seen to have been successful, my uncle and cousin packed up their *jholas* and left. This is when the main party arrived.

The price negotiations started at a lower level than the previous time, and given the seller's psychological state, started going lower. The deal was finally concluded under the cover of a coir basket, lest others get to know about the low price. We were thrilled, and so was Pradumna Uncle, the family entrepreneur, beaming from the cover of a nearby tree.

6

A Visit to Bodh Gaya: India's Race Against China

Karma yagna se jeevan ke
Sapno ka swarg milega...
Kintu banega kaun purohit
Ab yeh prashna naya hai.

The sacrificial fires of action
Will reveal the heaven of our dreams...
But who will propitiate these fires?
Is a question that still remains.

– JAISHANKAR PRASAD

Friday, 2 January 1998

The fog was clearing up when we started onward from Lucknow. As the train approached the Ganges, the expanse of the Gangetic plains came into view. I thought of the one-rupee-coin my sister and I would hurl into the water when we used to cross the river during our childhood, as we travelled to and from Gorakhpur. I noticed a few other hands dangling from the windows of the train, offering their own silent token to this holy river.

We travelled across Bihar to arrive at Bodh Gaya. The train passed through the wandering grounds of the Buddha. Towards the north was Kapilvastu in Nepal, where Siddhartha was born. Towards the south was Sarnath where Lord Buddha first preached. It is also where the national emblem of modern India – the four lion motif of Ashoka – originated. Towards the west, as we approached Bodh Gaya was Kushinagar, where the Buddha left his body.

Mohit Joshi had travelled from Kathgodam, in the Kumaon foothills, to be with us on the train. At the time, he was in the final year at Sainik School in Kathgodam, although his parents lived nearby in Ranikhet. A poet at heart, also a die-hard Ayn Rand fan, Mohit represented the sensibility of a small-town individual with an intellect and a curiosity that would find him friends anywhere in the world. He dressed and spoke in a manner that was less polished than that of the students from Delhi or Mumbai, but it did not take him long to make friends among those on the train. His knowledge on a variety of subjects, and his curiosity, intrigued the participants. Mohit described his life in his hometown where he had got hold of his first Ayn Rand book from a tourist. He then found and rapidly devoured most of her other works. His fondness for Kishore Kumar songs, his *joie de vivre* and pride for the country were infectious. He was here on this journey as he had learned of the 'religion of wandering' from the writings of Dr Rahul Sankrityayan.

In a way, our wanderings were similar to the travels of Prince Siddhartha. As a young prince, Siddhartha eschewed the worldly pleasures of his palace and set out on a journey into the real world. He was so moved by the hardships of an ordinary life that he set out to meditate and think of a better way to comprehend reality.

We too wanted to think outside the confines of metro cities and comfortable conference rooms. Our search was for the real India, in the company of diverse young Indians. But this was a personal journey as well. Each participant would take home their own vision of India.

As we approached Bodh Gaya, there was a certain level of excitement and nervousness. To cope with this stretch of the railway line in Bihar, we took on board a group of Railway Protection Force officers who were there to safeguard against miscreants who boarded trains in search of a free passage.

We arrived in Bodh Gaya to find that we were short of one bus, but we all managed to get on board the available buses and reached our destination. The experience at the Bodh Gaya temple was marked by a certain stillness. We stood at the very spot where the Buddha attained Nirvana. The Bodhi tree still stands, under whose ancient relative the Buddha meditated before he attained Enlightenment. The Bodhi tree had a particular fascination for us. Our situation, thousands of years later, is somewhat similar. We were also attempting to answer some fundamental questions. India was looking for a social, economic and political framework that would allow it to take a new direction in its development.

The play of light and colour at Bodh Gaya was mesmerizing. Monks in the hundreds were making their way towards the statue of the Buddha and prostrating themselves in meditation. As evening approached, thousands of oil lamps and incense sticks burned in the foreground of the temple. A giant statue of the Buddha rose in the background, with thousands of candles casting a meadow of light at his feet. Very much like the visit to the Golden Temple, the group members spoke in whispers, lest it disturb this tranquil atmosphere.

Mohit was keen to interact with the monks who had converged there from all over the world, besides those from Dharamsala itself. There were monks from Tibet, Burma and Thailand. Mohit conversed with a young monk from Tibet, roughly the same age as him. The monk's purple robes and spiritual air were nicely offset by a pair of Reebok trainers. We were struck by how ideas that originated from this very location spread to the farthest corners of Asia. In ancient times, when travel within the country itself was difficult, the Buddha's message went forth across the high mountains and the seas to influence distant civilizations.

We were conscious of India's growing collaboration and competition with China. Our discussions focused on what was unfolding in China, with whom we share a long border. How would this impact India? And how could both countries benefit from this interaction?

Our group discussed the enormous progress China had made since 1979. Under an economic liberalization drive led by Deng Xiaoping, China was unshackled from the straitjacket of orthodox Communist ideology. We discussed numerous areas where China has made remarkable progress since then. Studying and contrasting this progress with our own journey of development was crucial, as the scale and speed of the developmental process in India can only be matched by that of China.

It was interesting to note that China, so long isolated from the outside world, could manage to catch up so quickly and change its mindset once it decided to pursue economic growth. It seemed to show a certain pragmatism that was innate in the Chinese character.

India was more introspective, emphasizing the spiritual over the material world, and less practical and more philosophical perhaps.

Our discussions focused on the historical and socio-political impact this philosophical background had on the people of China and India. We analysed how this thought process has shaped development principles in both these nations as we know them today. China, a nation never very comfortable with competing ideas, took to Communism when it saw this as a bulwark against the grinding poverty that it faced. In an age where the middle kingdom was struggling to find its centre and purpose, China required a shock as great as the Communist system to shake it out of lethargy.

We discussed the success of China under the Communist regime and its emergence as a nation of freewheeling entrepreneurs. When Communism was discredited as an unsuccessful economic model, Chinese leaders led by Deng turned to the West.They opted for a system of economic growth with an emphasis on industrialization that had been successful in North America and western Europe. Was this a sustainable model for a nation with a population of more than a billion people? To develop a nation as large as China, a more original approach may be required. An approach that recognizes that the industrial development model, successful in Europe and North America, may not be sustainable in the long run on such a large scale, given its emphasis on intensive use of non-renewable resources and its effect on the environment. The same can be said for India.

There are many virtues to applaud in China today, but originality is not one of them. China's political system is straining against a world where technology and communication are making it difficult to keep a lid on the human need for freedom. India needs to study this model of development but be discerning in what it learns from this giant towards the north. China may have staked too much on conformity and industrialization.

On the train, the *azad gaon* and *azad nagar* groups were clear that India had a lot to learn from China in terms of infrastructure development. The special economic zone of Shenzhen helped propel economic reform in a big way and it has emerged as a powerhouse of growth. The power of the People's Liberation Army in ensuring that a country as large as China remains protected has little precedence. But the biggest lesson from China is its belief in itself.

While India's confidence has been battered by many years of occupation, China has stood resolute, isolated but erect nevertheless. When the Indian economy was being shaped to fulfil the demands of England, China still looked at the outside world with disdain. The Opium Wars and the Treaty of Nanjing confirmed the true interests of western powers towards the Chinese. In contrast, India lost its self-confidence during British occupation. A nation once proud of its philosophy, its heritage, constantly looked to the outside world for approval. In that respect, we must learn from China. If India is to think for itself, sweep away some of the systems which are still a hangover from its colonial past, it must alter the way it perceives itself.

But this self-confidence should not reject, negate or isolate itself from novel ideas just because they are foreign. We wanted a positive India, one which listened and was not insecure about adopting new modes of development. We felt India was well-equipped to take on this task. It had a pluralistic tradition, it was familiar with the global economy, and had an affinity to English which has become a key link language globally. In effect, it had tools to communicate with the world at large. However, external ideas had to be examined and adapted to our environment before they were implemented. Like Professor Dhar's innovative refrigeration project in Almora, or Bunker's solar-powered night schools, we needed to adapt these ideas to local conditions.

During our conversations, the environment and sustainable development group, in particular, expressed their concerns about the environmental challenges China and India would have to confront in the future. We were aware that numerous statistics stressed that the current industrial developmental model was unsustainable for both these nations. The early signs of environmental degradation were visible in cities like Delhi, while the booming car sector in China was putting enormous pressure on the transportation infrastructure and finite energy sources. In 2005, China on its own used 26 per cent of the world's crude steel, 32 per cent of its rice, 37 per cent of the world's cotton and 47 per cent of the world's cement. The industrialization of Europe led to the search for new natural resources. Energy hungry China and India, if they solely focused on industrialization, could trigger another round of economic colonization. The scramble for resources in Africa by China is an early indication that this is beginning to happen.

With a population of more than a billion, does India have to subscribe to the same developmental models as the West? Can India take a fresh look at the development process at a time when the western world is also struggling with an industrial hangover? In 2006, the *Stern Review* issued by the British government dramatically questioned the very models that led to the twentieth century success stories of Europe and North America. How do we benefit from the obvious advantages of an economic system which rewards merit and hard work, but refrains from rushing to adopt a development model just as it is beginning to get dated?

William Bernstein, in the *Birth of Plenty*, which is an enquiry into the origins of modern prosperity, talks of four key factors which powered an economic surge in seventeenth century Holland and England. While the technological innovation of the steam-engine was a necessary precursor, this was only one of the four factors. The other three factors were the right to property, the spirit of enquiry, and the availability of capital. This, in turn, led society to be powered by an 'abundance mentality', resulting in the social and political changes that helped the West take the lead.

If Indians have traditionally valued the spiritual and intellectual over the physical, information technology and a knowledge economy offer us a historic opportunity to redefine abundance. If India has to create an 'abundance mentality', we felt that it would be difficult to achieve this on simply a physical plane. We have to explore and redefine abundance in intellectual and human capital terms. Abundance is relative and depends on what an individual, a family or a nation cherishes most. Bigger is not always better, it is not necessary to own a large gas-guzzling motor car just to show that one is high up in the social order.

It is no coincidence that over the past three decades, the value generated through intangible assets has grown exponentially relative to that of physical assets. These intangible assets are largely the result of intellectual efforts in technological innovation in the field of computer science, and lately biotechnology. These intangible assets are also reflected in the value attributed to brands and creative processes. The premium paid for intangible assets is reflected in the large market capitalization of companies such as Microsoft in the US, GlaxoSmithKline in the UK, Novartis in Switzerland, Infosys or Ranbaxy in India. These companies have the capability to successfully deploy intangible assets such as human resources, process expertise, technology and brands to create enormous value.

The US economy and that of western Europe is also shifting to a service economy. Even in the manufacture of industrial products such as cars, the proportionate cost of software often exceeds that of hardware. This is a strategic trend that will take some time to impact our daily lives. India is already seizing this opportunity and if it succeeds in taking the lead in this area, it can compete in a far more favourable fashion with the rest of the world.

India has an abundant future if one takes this point of view. On the other hand, if progress is perceived in the form of large gas-guzzling cars, glass buildings, or worse still, giant shopping malls as in North America or Europe, then India with a dense population and scarce energy reserves will only see scarcity. Scarcity as seen in the days of the licence raj, leads to distrust, friction and ultimately lack of integrity. The battle for an integral India would be lost.

China is fast becoming an adjunct to the rest of the world as it is an extension of an industrial supply chain. India, in contrast, is an extension of an intellectual supply chain where the chances of differentiation and competition are far greater. India also has a greater market reach, as the potential for remote service provision is far greater than that of product manufacture. The chances of China outdoing the industrial West in manufacturing are less likely. There is a greater chance of India emerging as a front-runner in the emerging knowledge and service-based industries. The answer, we felt, lies in a strong national effort in this direction, by utilizing and drawing from our existing expertise in this area.

The growth in knowledge-based industry is not limited to IT-related areas alone but extends to biotechnology and to business services. There are possibilities in the field of medicine, where India has a pool of well-qualified scientists and doctors. The agricultural sector holds promise as advances in the field of horticulture, genetics and computer science are converging as never before. But the common requirement in these emerging industries is to use intellect, creativity and innovation, not merely massive factories. That is India's passport to success, and that is also our main differentiating factor and strategy to compete with China.

However, with only a 3 to 5 per cent expected GDP from software industries, and an even lower percentage of employment from these sectors, how can we speak of solving India's bigger problems through software and knowledge industries?

Walt Rostow, in his book *The Stages of Economic Growth: A Non-Communist Manifesto,* defines five stages as the key moments of an economic take-off. As an aircraft accelerates along the runway then lifts off, so does an economy about to expand rise quite steeply. Normally, this economic take-off typically occurs in a single critical sector, or at the most, in two. It was cotton in Britain. In France, Germany, Russia and the US, it was the railways, in Sweden it was timber and iron ore mines. In each case, the key sector darts forward, modernizing rapidly. The speed of its growth and modern technological advances are precisely what distinguish this process from previous growth phases. The industry that shoots ahead, increases its output, improves its technological skills, organizes its marketing and thus creates a value-added competence which then stimulates the rest of the economy.

While it is true that the so-called IT service industries, software, Business Process Outsourcing (BPO) and biotechnology industries on their own cannot power Indian growth, they have helped the Indian economy by being a lead sector. The use of steam power to release water from mines led to the creation of James Watt's steam engine, which transformed mobility and created the railways, transport and the steamship industries. Similarly, the IT services and biotechnology industries are starting to transform the way India performs in other spheres of economic and non-economic endeavour.

The government has to continue to encourage manufacture as it offers broader employment opportunities. However, for various reasons, some cultural, others related to our economic history, we still lag behind in this field. Having been part of the manufacturing and industrial world for eight years, I have witnessed this at close quarters. While working with Schlumberger, an oilfield services company, my first posting was in North Yemen. I was supervising rig operations on the edges of the Rub' al Khali, in the empty quarter of North Yemen. People of eight different nationalities were working together on the project. The Thai and Tunisian derrickmen demonstrated all the mechanical dexterity that was needed to operate the 90-foot-high derrick. The Dutch driller was adept at sending pipes thousands of feet down in search of oil. The French rig superintendent was an organizational whiz. But the doctor was Indian, the accountant was Indian, and the IT person was also Indian. Even in our regional headquarters in Singapore, Indians dominated in the accounting and IT department.

Archaic employment laws and restrictive bureaucratic rules have stunted the growth of the manufacturing sector in India. We should accelerate our efforts in this important area for there is no such thing as a pure knowledge economy, just as there was no such thing as a purely industrial economy. But if national energies are focused on developing the IT sector, biotechnology and agro-industries, we will be able to use our expertise in these fields to stimulate other areas, including the manufacturing sector.

Our discussions on the train threw up different views on the strategic relationship between India and China. My personal view remains that China and India will be natural adversaries in Asia. On the surface, we may appear to be on good terms, but geo-politically, competition is unavoidable, especially as it relates to energy resources. This competition will exist in a number of fields over the next fifty years. But this can be a healthy rivalry as compared to our unnatural obsession with Pakistan over the past many decades. This competition can spur both India and China onwards, instead of their remaining tethered to old differences.

The heads of states of China and Pakistan visited India in 2005 in quick succession. It was instructive to observe their travel itineraries. Wen Jinbao, the Chinese prime minister, started his visit in Bangalore wanting to visit the IT monuments of the future, while Parvez Musharraf, the Pakistani president, began his tour from a mosque, not missing an opportunity to make a symbolic, religious statement. India can continue to focus its national energies by engaging a neighbour where the dialogue remains negative, or choose to face a strategic competitor who can get the nation's competitive spirit flowing.

We felt that Pakistan continues to sway intellectually between its east, where modern nations are being built, and its west, where a resurgent Islam is trying to shape its national agenda. As a result, it remains confused and tentative in its interaction with India. For every euphoric bus journey across the border, every box of mangoes sent to the Indian prime minister, there has been a contradictory action: the confrontation at Kargil, attack on Parliament and other terrorist attacks that had their origins in Pakistan. Pakistan and modern Pakistanis need to make a clear choice about their national direction. Until such time, despite various 'summits', a positive engagement with Pakistan will remain a distant dream.

A Pakistani friend in London, a modern thinker, expressed a desire for a progressive framework in his country. He asked a mutual British friend, 'What are the three things that come to your mind when you think of India and Pakistan?'

For India our friend's reply was immediate, 'Bollywood, IT and a chaotic democracy.' As far as Pakistan is concerned, our friend answered slowly, 'Lawlessness, religion and a benign dictatorship.'

'See,' my Pakistani friend exclaimed in mock envy, 'this is what I hear from most!'

Unlike the post-independence leaders of India, the young participants on the train saw Pakistan as just another country. Pakistan is doing what other nations guided by religion are doing across the world – it is struggling. India has to leave it alone. Pakistan will find its own path and destiny. And if that destiny is Islamic, it may bring about clarity for Pakistan's own nation-building journey. But, most importantly, India should not be distracted by any negative interaction, and instead engage in a healthy competition.

In contrast, the race with China, we felt, provided a positive framework for development. It forms the basis for a healthy competition with a neighbour that has to be taken seriously, militarily, economically and even politically. But this is a secular competition where India stands to benefit.

China cannot be ignored militarily. India has the 1962 humiliation across the Himalayas as a reminder. The power game continues on various fronts. China has, for instance, aided Pakistan in its nuclear programme and it maintains influence over India's other neighbours to try and maintain a strategic edge.

Should this behaviour surprise India? Not in the least bit. We are the two biggest countries in Asia, and China has always been conscious of its strategic concerns. But for India, it poses a challenge to reorient its thinking. India has the wherewithal to engage on all these fronts. And in doing so, its national fibre will be tested, stretched and strengthened.

Economically, the Chinese are clearly in the lead. If they are the established factory of the world, India is its back office. Entrepreneurs on both sides are already fully engaged. India's National Institute for Information Technology (NIIT) already boasts of a hundred training centres in China. The white goods manufacturers from China are giving Indian manufacturers a run for their money. India's steel industry is benefitting from the building boom in China, while China is envious of India's leadership in the BPO sector, derived from its proficiency in the English language. China is trying to copy India's IT model; India is busy imitating Chinese free economic zones. We viewed this as a healthy competition and a tough fight but a growth-oriented one. In the long run, India will produce world-class industries as it competes, and sometimes collaborates, with a growing giant.

During our discussions, we recognized that on a political level, the outcome will be difficult to predict. China opened up its economy a decade before India did, but India's economic growth in the bustle of democracy though it is slower, may prove more consistent. China has used Communism as a bamboo path to steer large, mainly state-owned enterprises towards capitalism. India, in contrast, has a competitive market of freewheeling companies whose only road-block ironically is the government itself. One model for development may outdo the other in respect of growth, but in the emerging knowledge world, we felt that India is a more robust model. A world where technology and communication are making it difficult to keep political feelings suppressed, even the most authoritarian political setup will have to be democratized over time.

The Indian subcontinent has been host to a number of Chinese travellers, the most famous being Hsuan Tsang. This seventh century monk from Xian in China came to India in search of Buddhist scriptures. His disciples wrote about his journey in the form of a travelogue, as a semi-allegorical story that is well known in Chinese literature as *Journeys to the West*. In the book, Hsuan Tsang and his companion monkey travelled the Silk Route, crossed the Hindu Kush, braved the passes of the Himalayas, and tackled a number of allegorical monsters to find India, a land which was the fount of Buddhism. Hsuan Tsang returned to Xian rich in knowledge, and built a stupa which resembled those he had come across in India. He came to India not because of India's fabled wealth, which China itself possessed in abundance, but because he had heard that here, at the foot of the Bodhi tree, the Buddha had an insight that changed the way ordinary people perceived the world.

We felt it would be a mistake for India to lose its originality and intellectual resilience that have been its strength for centuries. It would be an even bigger mistake at this point, when the world is in search of a system that moves the economic framework beyond an industrial model.

7

Jamshedpur: Forged in Steel

The question isn't who's going to let me, it's who's going to stop me.

– Ayn Rand

Saturday, 3 January 1998

The city of Jamshedpur is a living testimony to the strength of one person's foresight – Jamsetji Tata, a visionary who founded the Tata group of companies. Although Jamsetji had passed away when this dream took shape, the seed he sowed in this small village in Bihar flowered into an enterprise which with its acquisition of Corus, is now a global player as well.

We arrived in Jamshedpur after travelling the length of Bihar without any major incident. The one incident worth reporting involved one of the organizers who also happens to be my cousin. Raju Bhaiya is known in the family for his courage and his ability to solve problems. He is a senior manager with the Grameen Bank in Gorakhpur and it was a pleasure to have him with us on the journey as a facilitator.

That morning, Raju Bhaiya got down at Ranchi as the train stopped for a short while to fill up on water. As he sat sipping tea on the cold winter morning, the train started moving without warning. As the train picked up speed, Raju Bhaiya ran alongside it and managed to get to the last coach, only to find the door locked. After hanging on and banging on the door unsuccessfully for quite some time, he was faced with a choice. He could travel by holding on to the door in the freezing wind, or traverse the outside of the carriage to safety. Being the person he is, he took the more dangerous route and made his way to the next door while holding on to the window bars. He succeeded in dodging onrushing telegraph poles and assorted dangers to finally gain entry as the train hurtled towards Jamshedpur.

The spirit of courage and enterprise are also what best describe Jamshedpur. Jamsetji was known for thinking the unthinkable, and then having the perseverance and energy to give shape to that vision. When others around him were uttering the word impossible, Jamsetji Tata was envisioning a large steel mill in a sleepy village. We were taken by the Jamshedpur welcoming committee to see a number of buildings and meet individuals who had contributed to the welfare of the city. We visited the Tata steel mills, where the words 'the will to work, the will to win' were emblazoned across the walls. The mill itself is seen as a model plant for industrial engineering, and has won praise for the way it has been planned. As we walked out of the factory, we witnessed the glow of a setting sun, lighting up this model township.

We were taken to the local sports stadium where we met archers – tribals from the region with a natural skill in the sport –

who had participated in the Asian Games. We ran a lap of honour with Shivnath Singh, the Indian Olympic runner and a medal-winner at the Asian Games. As we sprinted to the finish line, I felt energized. The combination of sports and leadership, change and enterprise was not accidental.

While we were unwinding at the stadium, Gautam Mukherjee, the chapter head of the Confederation of Indian Industries, gave us a scintillating talk on India's future. He spoke of a future that belonged to India and the USA. He said that these two countries have the agility and the creativity to adapt to the knowledge world. He highlighted the relevance of the Emotional Quotient as a key enabler of creativity and innovation. Intellect only took you so far, emotions allowed you to think differently and to relate to others within a wider group. While to some non-Indian participants on the train, Gautam's prophecy on the Indian IT industry sounded too optimistic, today his predictions are closer to being realized than he could have ever imagined at the time.

Our discussions on the train were focused on building institutions. How does one create sustainable institutions around a particular vision? And how could we learn from the Jamshedpur experience? For us, the *yatra* itself could be a starting point: we would focus on shaping young minds. These individuals would share a common vision in building successful institutions. Today, while the leisure societies of the western world seem beguilingly easygoing, there is years of tremendous effort hidden behind the appearance of ease. So it is with entrepreneurs – a great deal of hard work and at the end of it the joy of creating something of lasting value. As it would have been with Jamsetji.

This discussion manifested in an important debate on the train between the words 'fun' and 'creation'. The word 'fun' is relevant to a developed country where the average person is able to enjoy his or her personal space, family life, and the pleasures of a society where systems have already been established. In contrast, in a country like India, institutions are still in their infancy. Unless we create an ambience where 'fun' and 'creation' can be brought together, institutions will remain underdeveloped. As a nation, we have a long way to go before we can begin to enjoy the pleasures of that hard work.

Jamsetji was an early pioneer in 'building'. He gave vision to a company that is a market leader even today. The Tata Group provides employment and opportunities for thousands of individuals, and there are millions of others who indirectly benefit from its success. But Jamsetji had to strain every 'building muscle' in his body to bring his vision to life. In doing so, in creating the Tata Group, he was still having 'fun'. Tata Group also founded other institutions across the country. The Indian Institute of Science, where Jamsetji took on a sceptical Lord Curzon, who was reluctant to provide funding, was established as early as 1911 in Bangalore, and may have been the seed from which the current IT boom was born. The Tata Institute of Social Sciences in Mumbai and TERI in Delhi are other examples of successful institution-building. These institutes are rare examples of continuing excellence.

In over forty of the past sixty years, the task of building institutions was relegated to the state. Old institutions left behind by the British continued as before in the new dispensation. Preserving old norms became the order of the day, while any form of building outside these given boundaries was neglected. During the first forty years of independence, the Soviet style of central planning was easily accepted as this centralized thinking was suited to maintain the status quo. They were able to dictate old rules under the guise of a central plan, while true innovation which required listening and creating was neglected. Entrepreneurs who looked at innovation and creating fresh opportunities were sidelined, and the bureaucracy tightened its hold over our institutions.

When it came to building institutions, ordinary citizens were sidelined. While democracy gives people the right to vote, the right to participate in building institutions is a far more important prerogative. Freedom to vote can only act as a medium to vent frustrations. 'Freedom as democracy' has to be exercised by creating new institutions. Jamshedpur is such an example: amidst the poverty of Bihar stands a model township. The town is well planned; it has vast and well-maintained parks. The housing is well laid out; schools and hospitals are well funded and competently staffed. But even during our visit, the town was falling under siege from Patna. This was evident in the constant disputes between the town planning committee of Jamshedpur and the 'durbar' in Patna.

To build successful institutions, we discussed, the new generation will have to fight the existing rigid systems. They will have to build new institutions despite the limited resources of a growing nation. They will have to battle against a mindset where coping with the present takes precedence over the future.

As we boarded the train that night for Kolkata, we noticed a subtle change among the participants. The storming, forming and norming phase of our group was behind us, and now, the participants had gradually started taking over the running of the train. Even the few sceptical organizers were now fully engaged. The various functions of organizing the train were handed over to the participants. A facilitator in each compartment took over the daily roll call. It was conducted by a lead participant, and then reported over walkie-talkies to Colonel Patil, who was responsible for making sure that everyone was on board before the train departed from any station. The camera team by then had two volunteers who were on auto-pilot, ensuring that filming took place according to schedule. One of the participants was overseeing the catering. Others took on the responsibility of ensuring that the train was kept clean and that supplies were taken on board when required.

On popular request, we had also added one more point to our seven-point agenda. This *yatri* group was charged with organizing the next *yatra*. Participants in this group came to the conclusion that the *yatra* should be an annual event, or at the very least, could take place once in two years, and in this process become a sustainable institution in itself.

Women participants were particularly active. Almost 45 per cent of the train consisted of women. This had surprised us initially but we readily welcomed this turnout as we perceived women to be key agents of change. A number of these women participants were in charge of their respective compartments. Others were involved with the groups where they played a role in creatively presenting their findings. Deepali, who had been involved in the sponsorship drive, was responsible for sending the daily report that was to be published in the *Times of India*. Shefali was in charge of organizing Frank Worth and his motley camera crew. Sudeshna, who represented a Pune-based charity, was leading her contingent of street children with aplomb. Some of the participants like Juhi, Neha, Deepa, Durga, Gitanjali, Poonam and others were particularly active within the groups. And Purva, of course, was our protagonist in the film.

In Bodh Gaya, a film crew from BBC India also joined the train, anchored by Rahul Bose, who has achieved acclaim as a mainstream Bollywood actor. Rahul was making a documentary for *Style*, where he presented national events on BBC India. Rahul was an engaging personality and was drawn to the concept of the journey. He has subsequently established himself as an artist who can perform as easily in the genre of commercial cinema as that of offbeat cinema.

Rahul and his team, right from Bodh Gaya to Kolkata, were able to capture the essence of the journey. They joined in the impromptu discussions that had become the *yatra*'s central feature. One such discussion was the debate on environmental issues. We talked about how to balance growth while encouraging sustainable development. Rahul surprised us by his understanding of these issues and the insights he offered.

The local press also covered our journey well. The journey got national coverage on Doordarshan, Star TV, Zee TV, BBC and most national and local papers. The articles were encouraging, and somewhat curious to see whether we would succeed.

A controversy developed in the planning phase of the *yatra*. Originally, one leg of the journey had been planned to East India. Since the East is often left out of the national dialogue, we were very keen to ensure that our train passed through Assam. During the course of discussing the itinerary with a journalist, I had alluded to the fact that one concern at the time was the activities of the United Liberation Front of Assam (ULFA) in that area. I had all but forgotten this innocuous quote, when I found the daily carrying a headline on its second page: 'ULFA Threat Prevents *Yatra* from Going to Assam'.

We had our very own resident journalist on the train. Angshuman was a young student from Tripura and had travelled all the way to

Mumbai to participate in the train journey. Angshuman had taken to journalism at a young age, and wanted to pursue it as a career. Even during the journey, he had a gift for unearthing controversies which amused everyone. I remember him once edging up to me, wanting to clear a question he wanted to ask Madhur Bajaj during our visit to the Bajaj auto factory in Aurangabad. In the bonhomie of our interactive session, he wanted to pose an awkward question on a recent financial target announced by Bajaj Auto.

The task of putting our ideas and insights to paper was given to a select team of participants, with Karthik Rammana as its de facto head. For a Class XII student, Karthik had extraordinary passion and interest in the Indian foreign policy. He was therefore also a natural spokesperson for the group that represented India and the globe as part of our seven-point agenda. His views were radical. He had visions of converting the Ministry of External Affairs into a ministry where more attention and diplomatic resources were diverted to focus on external trade. This group started compiling the thoughts and recommendations of various groups in the form of a 'Manifesto of Young India for the Future'. It took an effort to compile and synthesize the discussions on the seven-point agenda, including the *azad gaon* and *azad nagar* groups. Each group leader had to interact with Karthik and his team. The team would then note down details and refine them on a clunky Toshiba laptop that had survived two weeks of the train journey. Our intention was to present this manifesto to the president at the Republic Day parade on 26 January 1998.

Karthik observed and later commented on how he had to reconcile diverse points of view while compiling the manifesto.

During one of the discussions, after listening to the group debate at length on population policy, one of the participants kept coming back to the issue of illegal immigration from Bangladesh since he came from the eastern region, where this is an emotive issue. He felt that other developmental issues were secondary in comparison to this immediate problem. This seemed a practical nuisance to Karthik at the time. Our minds were on loftier goals. But on reflection, Karthik understood that others saw the issues faced by India very differently.

Our discussions that formed the basis for the manifesto were not systematic, neither was the end product perfectly formed. However, everyone learned from the process. As each group presented their ideas to the rest of the team, these were refined through interaction. The first set of presentations took place by the time we reached Kolkata, and a second presentation was planned in Aurangabad at the Bajaj auto factory.

The manifesto identified five vital points necessary in building the India of tomorrow, and two additional groups focused on the infrastructure in the villages and cities. The population control group recognized that with 300 million additional births anticipated by 2025, India would see a cataclysmic change unless we did something about it. The manifesto tackled this problem with short- and long-term remedies. Participants were not shy to suggest that as a short-term measure, contraceptives be distributed along with cigarette packs. Long-term solutions involved addressing cultural and developmental factors that were hurdles in population control.

The environment and sustainable development group pointed out the dangers of following a path of development that exploited nature. Discussions ranged from waste dumping, sanitation and sewage treatment, to deforestation and global warming. 'In spite of her late arrival into the industrial age, India is almost on the verge of repeating all the mistakes of the industrial nations,' they wrote.

Agro-industries and entrepreneurship, the third group, created an action plan whereby agro-based industries would provide meaningful employment to the 65 per cent of Indians who lived in rural areas. They envisioned gram panchayats supporting agro-based industries which would focus on providing better access to villages and neighbouring markets. Their proposal included methods to start agro-based businesses and they identified resources to achieve these objectives.

The India and the globe group supported the need to be far more open to new ideas, as long as we tailored them to suit our circumstances. At the same time, they argued that we had to project our own culture. With six forms of classical dance, three streams of classical music genres, and a variety of food and diverse cultural styles, India had a lot to offer the world. However, India's contribution was still marginal in respect to the exchange of ideas taking place across the world. But they also accepted that 'India has a lot to learn from the various aspects of international culture. One area where a lot can be learnt is management'. The India and the globe group also discussed geopolitics and globalization. 'The collapse of the Soviet Union and the liberalization of the previously "closed" economies has drastically restructured international relations and ushered in "globalization".' Their understanding of globalization seems to me to be way ahead of its time. Globalization may be defined as a phenomenon whereby governments and their peoples develop stronger political, economic and cultural bonds.

Finally, the values group discussed the importance of truth, honesty and integrity, values which would have to underpin any national effort if the foundations of the nation were to be strong. They suggested, 'We need to be proud of our heritage, but this pride must also include acceptance of the fact that we need to change and assimilate positive aspects from other nations and cultures.' An obvious example was that of corruption, which had to be curbed.

The *azad gaon* and *azad nagar* groups crafted a vision for the future of rural and urban India. Both groups divided their goals for development into different categories – village industries, energy, water management, transport and communication, sewage and drainage. The *azad nagar* group discussed the Build Operate and Transfer (BOT) concept as a way of improving the infrastructure in India. And this was five years before the Noida toll highway, near Delhi, based on the BOT concept was conceived. The manifesto not only documented this vision, it also assessed the resources required to achieve their vision. As Subhashish Sarkar, a member of the *azad gaon* group, later remarked, 'How easy it was to ridicule and criticize, how difficult to construct and even envision a positive change.'

While the end product crafted on a train, with little access to primary or secondary research, was good, the process of thinking about the future itself was the most important outcome. As a group, we wanted to shape a positive future, not just celebrate the past. Our debates and the involvement of leaders like Bunker Roy, Kiran Bedi, Mark Tully and others allowed for a rich process of thought and enquiry. Our manifesto was based on action; participants not only suggested ways in which to implement ideas, they also pledged to take action. The environment and sustainable development group pledged: 'We resolve that personally involving ourselves in efforts to curb pollution will be our most significant contribution.

These efforts include cutting down on emission rates by using public transport, reducing garbage generated, and implementing basic measures like switching off unwanted lights etc., which are often ignored.'

The catering staff were the first to see this resolution put to practice. One afternoon, after a laborious morning cooking breakfast and organizing a packed lunch, one of the catering staff collected the vegetable peels in a small sack with the intent of disposing it in the gap between the train and the platform. A *yatri* from the environment and sustainable development group, seeing this, stomped over and reprimanded him for his behaviour. From then on, garbage disposal was organized at the appropriate points.

One facilitator, Keith Jackson, in particular, provided a very different perspective to our discussions with the eye of an outsider. Keith came to know about our project through his daughter Bridget. He had recently retired from business and volunteered to raise funds in the UK. He then got so taken in by the concept that he decided to join us on the train from Delhi.

Keith, while often frustrated by the lack of process in our discussions, got involved with the agro-industries and entrepreneurship group. He was puzzled by the discrepancies in India. He saw our youthful and positive train making its way through swathes of poverty. The task of finding a way out of this poverty and into a developed world excited as well as daunted him. He was often baffled by our optimism in the face of the obvious challenges faced by India. But like most outsiders, he was touched by the journey. He recognized that our discussions reflected a unique level of passion and enthusiasm. He also recognized that while this idealism may not change India, we were laying the first flagstone on the path to making a difference. He was impressed by the advances in the IT industry, but wanted us to face the poverty in India as well. As he had the dispassionate view of an outsider, he became a strong sounding board for our ideas.

Gautam Mukerjee's talk at the Jamshedpur sports stadium had inspired a number of participants. Like Gautam, we recognized that we were on the threshold of a great leap forward. The only force that could stop us from making this leap would be Indians themselves. The demolition of the licence raj in 1991 saw India emerge as a nation where the 'statist' powers of the government were beginning to recede. Individuals who wanted to work hard, who could take risks to follow their dreams had every chance of success, just as Jamsetji, after whom this city was named, had demonstrated.

On the way to Ahmedabad.
(Photo credit: Vipul Sangoi, Raindesign)

Participants sit in rapt attention during an interactive session in Tilonia. *(Photo credit: Vipul Sangoi, Raindesign)*

Bunker Roy taking part in our discussions on the train.
(Photo credit: Vipul Sangoi, Raindesign)

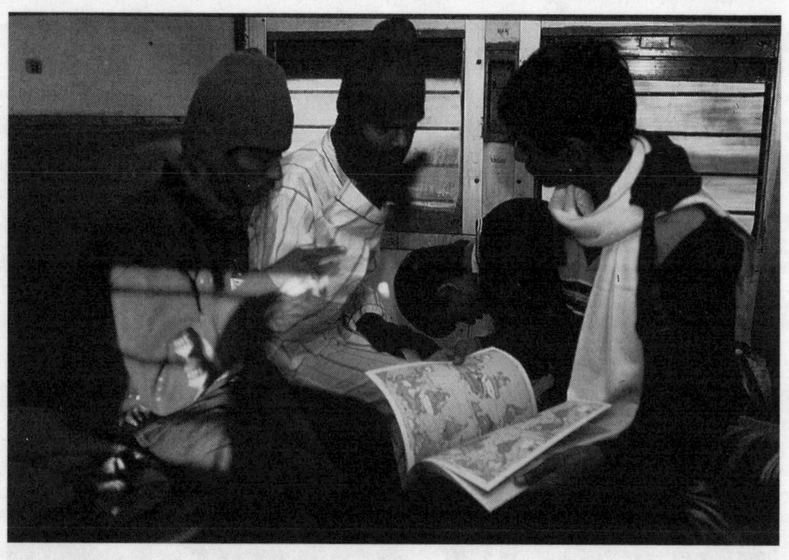

Participants share their ideas on the train.
(Photo credit: Vipul Sangoi, Raindesign)

The train pulls into Delhi.
(Photo credit: Vipul Sangoi, Raindesign)

On the steps of the Rashtrapati Bhavan.
(Photo credit: Vipul Sangoi, Raindesign)

En route to Bodh Gaya.
(Photo credit: Avinash Pasricha)

Meeting Anna Hazare in Ralegaon Siddhi.
(Photo credit: Avinash Pasricha)

8

Magical Kolkata: Risk and Adventure

When you are in search of honey, you must expect to be stung by bees.

– Kenneth Kaunda

Sunday, 4 January 1998

We left Jamshedpur and our journey took us eastwards to Kolkata. Crossing the Subarnarekha river on the outskirts of Jamshedpur, we left the Chotta Nagpur plateau for the lush green paddy fields of the gangetic delta in Bengal. We were to stop in Kolkata for two days to take on new participants. We also wanted to give ourselves a well-earned rest prior to the journey back to Mumbai.

Gitanjali Banerjee, a participant from Dehra Dun, had contacted us on seeing the *Times of India* article by Jerry Pinto. She took an avid interest in outdoor activities, having grown up near the Forest Research Institute in Dehra Dun. Her essays demonstrated a forward-looking vision for India with a particular passion for India's flora and fauna. She was part of the *azad gaon* group which combined her interests with that of sustainable rural development. On this particular leg of the journey, Gitanjali and Aradhana, another participant, managed to convince us that if they travelled in the guards' compartment, it would allow them to alert us immediately if the train made an unscheduled stop. They equipped themselves with walkie-talkies and spent the best part of the day refining their ideas on village development with Ram Singh, the guard.

The train had been our home for two weeks by then. Despite the fog in the North, the railways had made every attempt to prioritize our passage. We noticed a sense of efficiency in the railways. Despite the obvious strain of carrying sixteen million passengers daily and two million tonnes of goods every day across the country, trains were running well, water was provided when needed, and drivers and guards showed up with surprising punctuality. Starting from the chairman of the railway board down to stationmasters, there was a professionalism which contrasted with the 'clerical' and 'hands-off' approach I have seen in other government departments. My uncle, Dhananjaya, then a senior officer in the railways, after failing to gently deter me from the project, had thrown his weight behind the event. As children, we had seen that he never strayed very far from a phone, lest an operational issue require his input. He was frequently on top of the departure times of trains, and often personally cross-checked running schedules with the stationmasters. This professional competence and zeal seemed to be echoed in the entire organization.

Our train was to stop at Howrah, but it instead was made to stop at a nearby station at Santragachi. This important suburban station proved extremely inconvenient for us as it required a forty-five-minute commute for us to reach Howrah station where our buses had assembled.

The first day was particularly nerve-wracking. As we prepared to make our way from Santragachhi to the Howrah station, we were unaware of the trials that lay ahead. We had to coordinate over two hundred people, including ten handicapped participants and some who were nearing sixty in our group of facilitators. We had four walkie-talkies but not much else to usher our team along. Having bought local train tickets with some inconvenience, we waited as train after train approached the station and left bursting at the seams. After a long wait, we finally decided to get onto a train whatever be the circumstances. And we finally did succeed.

We were left hanging from the windows of a train, clutching our bags and ensuring that other participants were out of harm's way. We hung from iron grips alongside the coach doors with a toe-hold on the footboard, unsure if everyone had boarded the train. Our walkie-talkies were clenched between our teeth as we tried to shout instructions as the participants boarded the train all together. Not one, but two layers of humanity cushioned the compartments. Other trains whizzed past in both directions, we were inches away from the telegraph poles along the tracks. Howrah, only forty-five minutes away, seemed far away. All that was needed was a hand or a foot to slip and lives would have been in jeopardy. In the scheme of things, it was seemingly a small incident, but we were reminded of the precariousness of our larger journey by the episode.

Conscious risk-taking, physical and intellectual adventure were central to the journey. We could have had our discussions in the air-conditioned environs of a seminar hall. However, the concept of a trans-India train journey attracted natural risk-takers. These participants were excited by the sheer thought of going out, meeting people, exploring the real India, and taking risks while doing so. We recognized that this sense of adventure was central to any building effort.

I was inspired to travel at a young age by the explorer and writer Rahul Sankrityayan. He wanted young Indians to adopt the 'religion of wandering' or *ghumakkadi ka dharma*. In his essay *Athatho ghummakad jigyasa* he wrote, 'If your father says not to, your mother prevents, your sister admonishes, your brother refrains you from travelling, ignore them; explore the world.' Having ventured into Tibet on his own, Rahul Sankrityayan had travelled up through China and on to Russia. His writings were popular in the early twentieth century. Inspired by him, and my adventurous cousin, Vijay Bhaiya – who introduced me to Rahul Sankrityayan – I travelled to the distant corners of India at an early age.

The Youth Hostel Movement of India also introduced me to the joys of trekking and adventure sports. Its motto 'wandering one gathers honey' echoes the sentiments of Rahul Sankrityayan. The Youth Hostel's National Himalayan Trekking Programme led in part by Vijay Bhaiya, allowed me to experience the beauty of Jammu and Kashmir when I was fourteen years old. Climbing the snow-clad Margan Pass in the Pir Panjal range into the valley of Kashmir, walking across the nearby paddy fields gave me a view of India hardly possible from a class-room window. During the trip, I befriended Maya, Mahesh, Vibha and sixty-year-old Bapu from Sholapur who was always the first up a steep incline. They gave me a glimpse of distant towns which were unknown destinations at the time.

Discovery and adventure are a state of mind. Adventurers believe that another and a better world can be found. Adventure requires a certain 'youth of mind'. In a world where idealism is being smothered early in life, a spirit of adventure revives it. It is easy to deride it, but at the heart of human endeavour lies a sense of adventure that gets us out of bed every morning to explore the world.

Adventure and risk-taking are closely tied to building a young country. It is a process that requires individual effort. It requires an atmosphere where these qualities are celebrated. The spirit of adventure often manifests itself as a physical journey such as our *yatra*, but more often than not, it is an intellectual and an emotional journey which requires people to break new ground in the field of relationships and ideas. The incident at Santragachhi reminded us that we were taking physical and intellectual risks by being part of a journey that was the first of its kind. We became braver as we observed the courage of others. We became supportive of each other when we recognized that the path we strode was difficult, but that we shared a common goal. Most importantly, by seeing new places and meeting new people, we were influenced in our thinking and in our behaviour in ways more powerful than by reading a book or by taking a course in a university.

The individuals we interacted with during our travels affected us more than the places we visited. The stories of blind participants Radheyshyam and Akhtar spoke of courage. Shubham, the street child, took enormous emotional risks in taking up the challenge to change his circumstances. The bravery of the handicapped girls from Pune who came along on a non-stop twenty-two-day journey was a display of courage. Karthik's ability to question his famous grand-uncle in public on an issue he was passionate about is yet another example of intellectual courage.

Can adventure and entrepreneurship be linked? Is there a link between shaping young minds, creating new institutions and taking personal, intellectual – and sometimes – physical risks? Those who came on a non-stop twenty-two-day trans-India journey understood that there were risks involved. We saw that the participants were idealistic, open to new ideas, and perhaps prepared to take risks in their daily lives as well. Would these participants nurture social institutions, create businesses, encourage team work? Probably yes. Would they then have the perseverance to keep going until they saw those institutions flourish? If so, they will succeed in creating the tryst with destiny our founding fathers envisaged.

This spirit of adventure combined with the willingness to take personal risks has led to the creation of a number of leading companies and social institutions. K.V. Kamath at ICICI Bank, Narayan Murthy at Infosys, Azim Premji at Wipro, M.S. Oberoi at the Oberoi Group, Lakshmi Mittal at Mittal Steel and many others are examples of successful entrepreneurs in the business world; others like Ila Bhatt at SEWA, Bunker Roy at Tilonia, Mohammad Yunus at Grameen Bank, and Anna Hazare at Ralegaon Siddhi are apt examples in the social field. These individuals often risked their personal credibility, stood up for their beliefs, persevered and eventually succeeded in what they set out to do. When Lakshmi Mittal focused his energies on an acquisition-led growth strategy, steel prices were low and plummeting. His risk paid off, and when steel prices surged, Mittal Steel was well positioned to make a bid for its biggest rival, Arcelor. Today Arcelor Mittal is the world's number one steel company. When Mohammed Yunus started down the road to micro-finance, traditional financial institutions sniggered at him. I guess a Nobel Prize is enough to silence them. These individuals were looking for something different, they were setting their own path.

India's founding fathers, and the generation that followed, demanded individuals to look at nation-building in the form of a 'public service'. While some of these individual efforts have led to the creation of prominent institutions, they robbed individuals of their personal sense of adventure.

Vikram Sarabhai and A.P.J. Abdul Kalam are examples of personal risk-takers who served India in 'mission mode'. Both dedicated their lives to achieve excellence in space research and wider scientific research, and they took significant personal risks in doing so. A number of bureaucrats, politicians, army officers and public servants also fall in this category. But these are exceptional people.

The 'public service' method dictates where to take risks, what to do, and over time, robs the individual of his or her sense of personal adventure. While the 'temples of modern India' were built in 'public service' mode, sustainable nation-building, we felt, would be best achieved by awakening a sense of personal adventure in an individual or a group.

We finally arrived at Howrah from Santragachhi surprisingly intact, and our buses were waiting for us. Ina Puri had worked overtime to arrange an eclectic itinerary in Kolkata. Ina is a theatre personality and was intrigued by the *yatra.* She personally took charge of taking us through the city. On a more personal note, the parents of a friend, Somesh Khanna, ensured that our stay in Kolkata was comfortable.

Our first stop was the National Museum in Kolkata where its director, Shyamal Chakraborty, introduced us to one of the oldest museums in the world. He ushered us into the museum's auditorium and related its history and spoke to us about the ancient art and culture of India. But we also discovered that amongst the residents of Kolkata, the museum is known as *jadoo ghar*, or the house of magic. It houses a number of artefacts from across the country and from different parts of the world. But *jadoo ghar* also prompts visions of magic and mystery. The Asiatic Society, the pre-eminent Indian historical research body in the eighteenth century, was also located here. One wonders if the phrase *jadoo* also reflects the lens through which Indians and Orientalists viewed each other.

We were then taken to meet Veena Bhargava, a well-known painter from Kolkata. She allowed us inside her studio. As the *yatris* squeezed into her studio in two batches, the discussion turned to the pressure on young students in India to pursue science to the exclusion of the arts. Increasingly, the study of law, medicine, engineering, and similar technical fields are seen as a ready means of earning a livelihood, while pursuing a degree in arts is often considered insubstantial. Juhi, in particular, was speaking from experience. She had wanted to pursue a career in design, and to that end had persevered to take a degree in creative arts. She could easily relate to the ambience in that studio and contributed in a big way to our discussions.

We discussed that in an emerging economy such as India, creative arts had to complement the emphasis on science and the technical aspects of education. Science and technology provide us the tools to excel; the arts provide a context to choose the right direction. India needs to encourage creative and artistic talent alongside hard technological pursuits. The arts provide the right medium for projecting our culture, and in differentiating ourselves from the rest of the world. Institutes like the National Institute of Design, where Juhi was to continue her future studies, will be central to our creative impulse.

The discussion at Veena Bhargava's studio ended with a performance by Darshana Jhaveri, an internationally acclaimed dancer. Darshana Jhaveri is one of the leading exponents of Manipuri dance in India and has devoted her life to this art form. Her family learned this art from Guru Bipin Singh of Manipur. Living in Mumbai, the Jhaveri sisters have spent their lives promoting and propagating it across the world. On this day, Darshana Ben and her troupe performed at the Birla Auditorium for the participants.

Many years ago, during our visit to East India, Gauri and I had visited Guru Bipin Singh of the Manipuri School of Dance in Imphal. We experienced the richness of this ancient dance form first-hand. Guru Bipin Singh, surrounded by students from across the world, taught this art form in a simple building at the centre of the city. We wondered how this evolved and fluid art form nurtured in this remote region of India could gain a wider audience across the world. Darshana Ben has dedicated her life to be one such conduit.

Ina Puri, Veena Bhargava and Darshana Jhaveri were also individuals whose lives spoke of adventure and a willingness to take risks. In their own way, these three women had devoted their lives to something they felt passionately about. They were willing to take any risks and to surmount any obstacle that came their way. This sparked a debate amongst the *yatris* over the pursuit of one's passion as opposed to following a career where one worked to earn a mere living. We felt that individuals had to discover that passion for themselves. Once that passion was discovered, life would take on a deeper meaning and work would be more enjoyable.

Kolkata, and specifically the chaos at Santragachhi, had taught us the power of risk-taking. For those few minutes when lives were at risk, it brought into sharp focus what we were trying to achieve through the *yatra*. I believe it was no coincidence that we met three women in Kolkata – Ina, Veena and Darshana Ben – who had chosen passion over mundane existence and had taken risks to pursue their dreams.

Not everyone has that spirit of adventure; the willingness to take risks. If all young people in India turned into mavericks, there would be chaos instead of positive change in our country. But this journey was about leadership and change. It was organized deliberately to attract those who were able to catalyse change. By reaching out to 200 participants, our hope was that at least one hundred out of those would be able to change their lives and follow their dreams. And at least fifty out of those hundred would create or help create institutions which would help India prosper.

At this point in the journey, the groups were actively carrying on debates and were documenting their discussions. A few took the initiative to visit the local library in Kolkata to obtain reference material for the manifesto, and their story is also full of adventure. A group of eight participants arrived at the National Library expecting a warm reception to their noble cause. The librarian, however, refused point-blank to issue them any reading material. The group then withdrew, and after some consultation agreed that Gitanjali Banerjee should approach the librarian again. After some persuasive chit-chat, Gitanjali, speaking in Bengali, convinced the librarian to help them. The group then got so engrossed with their research work that they realized the lateness of the hour only at 4 p.m., when the train was about to depart. Frantic phone calls were made and the group finally managed to connect with one of the facilitators, who told them that they had to return forthwith or the train would leave without them. There was a bus strike in

Kolkata, so they took a rikshaw, then a ferry across the Hooghly, and finally a train to reach Santragachhi, only to find that the main party had still not returned from Howrah!

Their enthusiasm reminded me of our discussions while trying to raise funds for the journey with the honourable Human Resource Development (HRD) minister who chaired the Golden Jubilee Committee. Once we had succeeded in drawing participants, our focus shifted to the sponsorship drive for the journey. We had some seed funding from Azad Shivdasani, others like Raju Shete and Madhur Bajaj as friends had provided sponsorships for students, but we needed a major sponsor for the journey to complement Azad Shivdasani's generous promise of a grant from the Inlaks Foundation.

We were facing the challenges of an early stage entrepreneur. If we did not believe in the journey, others would not either. If, on the other hand, we took the project forward based only on our convictions and were unable to raise the full amount, it would be a letdown for all the participants. With no concession from the railway ministry, we were behind our funding target. This was the most stressful time for us. Having experienced the friction in Delhi, we decided not to depend on the largesse of the government to fund the project. Instead, we marketed the idea to various trusts and companies in the hope of gaining their support.

A key breakthrough came from Vikram Sakhuja at Coca-Cola. Vicky was a close friend from IIT Delhi. He had been the secretary of our hostel, although his real passion was for dramatics. When I explained the concept of the journey to Vicky, he was initially unmoved. He challenged us on the lasting benefits of this one-off event. My explanation to him was that this was intentional. As professionals engaged in our own busy lives, we were ill-equipped to devote time to a particular social cause on a sustained basis. Through this one-off journey in the fiftieth year of India's independence, we hoped to make a small contribution. Over the course of a number of discussions, Vicky grew convinced. He first coached us on how to sell the idea, and then introduced us to the relevant person at Coca-Cola. We made a passionate pitch and waited for a response. Those days in October 1997 were the darkest in the organizational saga.

Then, one morning, we got a call from Coca-Cola. They were ready to come on board as the main sponsor. Literally eight weeks before the journey was to commence, our perseverance had paid off. The majority of funds was more or less in place with Inlaks and Coca-Cola. Now, not only did we have the funds but we also had support from a large number of people who believed in the project. Finally, Colgate, led by Maitrey Kumar, also came on board as one of the main sponsors.

The Golden Jubilee Committee and the HRD ministry had also sanctioned a grant. However, just seven weeks before we were to embark on the journey, the grant was reduced significantly from the original amount. This was a major dent to our funds and had the potential to derail our project. I travelled to Delhi to meet with the HRD minister to convince him that this journey complemented other celebrations around the Golden Jubilee. In the half-hour session with the minister and his secretary, I argued that looking forward to celebrate India's fifty years of independence was as important as celebrating the past. I highlighted the fact that the journey would give young Indians a unique view of India. While the minister and his secretary listened to my point of view, they stuck to the grant at the reduced amount. As we parted at the end of the meeting, the secretary suggested we 'cut our suit to fit the cloth'.

Given this sudden turn of events, we were forced to curtail the journey. We had been keen to go around India, including Tamil Nadu and Kerala, to make sure this journey was a truly trans-national expedition, but that was not to be. We were forced to limit the journey and Visakhapatnam (Vizag) became the southernmost point of the journey.

After our visit to Kolkata, I moved from the organizer's coach to one of the boys' coaches. Often, the most interesting discussions took place at night and I wanted to listen in on them. Before the commencement of the journey, we had often wondered whether the participants would be able to take the physical strain of a non-stop twenty-two-day train journey. Barring the brief bout of tiredness experienced in Delhi after the first leg of the journey, fatigue and tiredness were left far behind as our train prepared for its southward journey from Kolkata.

9

South, Past Chilka: Wisdom and Values

Saints, I see the world is mad
If I tell the truth they rush to beat me
If I lie they trust me.

– Kabir

Tuesday, 6 January 1998

It was 2 a.m. In the darkness, we stumbled across the railway lines to the stationmaster's cabin in Santragachhi and spoke to the control-room at Howrah station on the phone. We wanted to be ahead of the Madras Express. 'Yes, we will be ready to leave at four in the morning,' I said. The stationmaster was not convinced. I turned to the local guard and did what we had done for the past two weeks – we showed him the letter from the chairman of the railway board. He spoke to his colleague and everything seemed in place.

After an hour's sleep, at 3:30 a.m., we asked for two volunteers to stay in the guards' compartment with walkie-talkies in hand. I kept one next to my bunk. Juhi and Sandeep volunteered and we saw them safely to the guards' compartment. Our instructions were for them to alert us if the train slowed down, as it would mean the Madras Express was overtaking us. The train moved out sharp at 4 a.m. The chairman's letter had worked. We slept soundly; we had managed to put ourselves ahead of the superfast Madras Express for which most trains were made to give way. For the next eight hours, we moved at breathtaking speed down the eastern coast of India with Juhi and Sandeep installed in the guard's compartment. Almost like the juggernaut of the nearby town of Puri, our train seemed unstoppable.

This stretch of the railway line hugging the eastern coast of India took us down the Kalinga territory, a kingdom which resisted repeated invasions by Ashoka. When Ashoka finally succeeded, circa 260 BC, he witnessed so much destruction that he forsook violence and became a Buddhist. We were speeding across fields which were once soaked with the blood of thousands of soldiers put to the sword by Ashoka before he took to Buddhism.

The sun was rising as we awoke to *Vande Mataram* and the sound of a fast-moving train. A vast expanse of water stretched to our left. At first, we thought it was the Bay of Bengal, but one could also see trees on the distant horizon. This was the Chilka Lake in Orissa, the largest saltwater lake in India. Its vast expanse stretched towards the horizons, placid and deep.

On this leg of the journey, our discussions in the common room were led by the values group, and our focus returned to the underlying cross-currents of culture that have shaped how India looked at itself and the world. At a certain time in history, India was described as *sone ki chidiya,* literally meaning a golden bird, because of its vast treasure of wealth. India traded with the rest of the world in spices, incense and luxury goods. Europe marvelled at its fabled wealth, and adventurers like Christopher Columbus mistakenly named entire tribes after it.

While India was regarded as a 'golden bird', what was less well known by explorers was its richness in the field of ideas. Religions such as Sikhism, Buddhism, Jainism found fertile soil in India. In the temporal and political sense, India provided the flexibility and space for people from other parts of the world to maintain their identities, for example, the Zoroastrians. The foreigner finds India confusing with its multitude of beliefs, while Indians who travel abroad are at ease with ambiguity. If the USA calls itself a melting pot where people are required to blend in physically and intellectually to become American, in India, on the other hand, diverse ideas are given the freedom to compete. We felt that this had enormous relevance in the knowledge era.

The group discussed how ancient Indians revered *gyana yoga.* It was believed that it is in complete devotion to knowledge (*gyana*), either through listening or through reading that one comes to the realization of the self. This philosophy is relevant now based on the remarkable developments in digital technology and the democratic explosion of commerce over the past three decades. The zero digit which was borrowed by the Arabs from India has found its way back to this land attached to a microchip. Now, through the power of the microchip, a device largely invented elsewhere, India seems to be rediscovering its long forgotten confidence.

A number of civilizations have used foreign inventions and adapted them to suit their own environment. As early as 1973, much before the Internet came into existence, the historian-philosopher, Sir Arnold Toynbee, in *A Study of History* predicted to the effect that the worldwide network of communications which the western civilization has installed for its own purpose is likely to find its historic significance in the familiar ironic role of being turned to account by unintended beneficiaries.

Indians are beginning to draw from their intellectual heritage and this has resulted in an economic flourish in modern India. This is starting to happen both in the provision of remote services and more recently in cultural fields as well. For example, Patanjali's *Yoga Sutras* gives a practical framework for self-improvement. It is very relevant for employees these days who spend eight hours in front of their computer screens.

We can also learn from the three *gunas* described in the *Gita.* These psycho-physical energy threads are qualities that are found in every human being. The three *gunas* are: *tamas* (dullness and inertia), *rajas* (the fire of desire and spiritedness) and *sattva* (pure intelligence and goodness). Indians run to an American university to pick up the latest in western thought, but we seldom make the effort to draw knowledge from the *Gita*, or seek wisdom from Thiruvalluvar in our own backyard.

As another example, we discussed Sufism which combined and reconciled the highest form of unitary Islam with the mysticism of the East. But Sufis have been rejected by the world as 'a band of fakirs'. I have visited the *dargah* of the Sufi saint Khwaja Moin-ud-din Chisti at Ajmer Sharif near Jaipur twice. On the first trip, my mother tied a ribbon at this shrine to seek a boon. She then dutifully went to retrieve the ribbon once her wish was fulfilled. The sense of universal love was palpable in the mosque. The big pot of food in the communal kitchen was full with the blessings of the saint.

On both occasions, I admired the energy and sense of community that the mosque exuded. We could enrich India's culture by adapting this mystic tradition to modern needs.

When India was labelled *sone ki chidiya* what people failed to see was that India's riches lay in its knowledge and diversity of ideas. To a westerner born and brought up with a different perspective, this contest of ideas was difficult to grasp. Therefore, India was treated as an exotic relic to be admired in a museum. Worse still, because Indians accepted this caged version of their past, we did not draw from the country's wisdom and genius to adapt it to the modern world. Scholars like Sir William Jones and James Prinsep in the late seventeenth and early eighteenth century perpetuated the 'golden bird' nomenclature with their 'discoveries' of Indian culture. Viceroys like George Curzon loved India, but like the Taj Mahal he so admired, India posed a challenge of 'presentation and preservation'. Indians today are singularly guilty of admiration rather than utilization. We glorify our past rather than make sensible use of it today, and for the world of tomorrow. The knowledge and service economy is asking us to free that bird and let it take wing.

On the one extreme there is blind admiration of India's past glory. I experienced a certain cultural rejection during one of the 'self-portrait' sessions on the train. When asked to present myself in the form of a symbol drawn on the flip chart, I stood unsure for a few moments. I then fluidly sketched myself as an arrow aimed at the eye of the fish, drawing upon Arjuna's prowess with the bow as recounted in the *Mahabharata*, or Rama's for that matter, in the *Ramayana*.

The character of Rama influenced me as I was growing up. I valued his serenity and his unflappable nature. Some of these influences are shaped by early experiences. While walking through villages in eastern U.P., I often found elderly villagers sitting outside their homes with a well-thumbed copy of the *Ramcharitmanas* at sunset. This scene has been played out in many parts of India through the centuries and has left an imprint on me. A facilitator in the audience later told me how disappointed she was that I had referred to Rama in my description. According to her belief, Tulsidas, Kabir, Kalidas, Nanak, Chishti, Ahura Mazda, Thiruvalluvar were not apt examples. Had I described myself in Shakespearean terms she may have empathized instantly.

Our train had slowed down. It was 11 a.m. and we ground to a halt at a small station in Andhra Pradesh. Within minutes our team accosted the stationmaster who informed us that we had to make way for the Madras Express to pass. The 'letter' for once did not persuade him. Juhi and Sandeep emerged from the guards' compartment red-eyed but elated. We had made good time in the past eight hours, the only issue being that as the train was moving extraordinarily fast, some of us had to do without a hot water bath.

Our makeshift bathroom had served us well over the past two weeks. To cope with the severity of the winters in the North, we had to make arrangements for hot water as well. We had constructed a large furnace made of clay and placed a large cauldron of water over it. Anyone wishing to take a bath had to mix water from the cauldron with cold water from the shower cubicles. This hot water contraption had not been entirely stable that morning as our train literally careened across the east coast of India chased by the Madras Express. Most participants went without a bath on that bone-rattling sprint towards the South.

The top brass of the Eastern Naval Command was waiting for us at the headquarters in Vizag. The Navy had organized a tour of submarines and destroyers for our contingent. We knew that further delays could throw our itinerary out of gear. Bathed or not, we needed to reach Vizag on time. The day went in persuading stationmasters to give us priority over other trains which were whizzing past at an alarming frequency. The culture as we moved south was perceptibly different. Every stationmaster we negotiated with was that much more considerate. They seemed more at ease, and their responses seemed much more considered.

As the train slowed down to a de-prioritized crawl towards Vizag, the values group spent the afternoon sharing their insights with other participants. They came to the conclusion that in a growing knowledge economy, values of honesty, truth, integrity, relevant in most ages, acquired a special significance. Trust and integrity were extremely important in the knowledge economy, be it in the IT, BPO, biotechnology or in the service sector. For such industries, group work, and the ability to deliver a promise to a customer was critical. The result of such services is not tangible; it is an intangible service. Howsoever concretely we quantify that service, we would have to lay our trust in the individual or team delivering it. If the laws of mechanics and property law shaped the conduct of nations in an industrial era, the new world of knowledge and service require a new personal code of integrity.

Despite the end of licence raj and the economic surge that came with it, India has continued to do poorly in its performance on fighting corruption. According to a survey in 2005, India has been rated to have one of the highest levels of corruption. In a Global Corruption Index, a survey of 133 nations conducted by Transparency International, India stood eighty-third in the world, alongside

Malawi. Finland, on the other hand, has been ranked as the least corrupt nation in the world. On the whole, the survey demonstrates that while Indian society preaches integrity, corruption is rampant. In a country where the population is exploding, competition for acquiring jobs and economic opportunities forces citizens to play the system rather than improve it.

Hazel, a Finnish student visiting Tilonia, decided to join us on Bunker's suggestion. As these discussions took place, she seemed most perturbed. India, with its diverse viewpoints, was confusing. Hazel was therefore very involved when the values group presented us with its framework which they called a 'tree of perfection'. The base of the tree and its trunk represented fundamental principles of truth and honesty that most societies live by. Each shoot from that trunk was a feature of that principle and each branch from that shoot embodied a set of behaviours which emphasized trust. The fruits of this tree represented goodwill.

Truth and honesty are a part of every culture, be it Finnish or Indian. Why then have some of these principles been so invisible in India recently, especially in a society that pays so much importance to spiritual and moral values? The values group felt that this was due to our increasing economic wants combined with a decreasing economic pie amidst a growing population. The average Indian is forced by economic circumstances to cut corners. This destroys trust and creates friction in each transaction, whether in the social sphere, within a family, in professional relationships or between the government and its citizenry. Families feud, companies resort to subterfuge, and most importantly, the gap between citizens and an all-pervasive government is filled with distrust. We felt that this lack of trust limits India's growth.

The values group came up with a simple solution to this situation: we needed to advertise champions of truth and integrity who could re-invigorate underlying trust in society, individuals who have fought a system that asks them to make constant compromises, individuals who have maintained their sanity and the fibre of the country by not yielding, and succeeded. However, these islands of integrity are submerged in a sea of 'rooftop corruption'. We buy newspapers that talk of a corrupt corporator rather than an honest one. Our instinct for lapping up the negative hinders us from observing those lamps of integrity that still burn brightly in India. In many ways, our *yatra* was about removing cynicism by meeting these Indians and believing in them. The values group was not speaking about these individuals in the abstract: some like Bunker Roy and Kiran Bedi had travelled with us, and others we were about to visit.

But technology is also providing citizens with a 'matrix of truth'. When we can use digital devices to zap information from computers, cellphones and television screens thousands of miles away that connect people and transfer information rapidly, transparency should be seen as a natural phenomenon. However, there are clashes with the old system, where it is considered important to quietly pay bribes and to use connections to help a company prosper. The Right to Information Act is finally coming to grips with this issue, but it will take some time to exorcize the ghost of the original Official Secrets Act.

Some months ago, I went to the land registry office in U.P. to get an affidavit attested and registered. The U.P. government has started computerizing all land records – a much needed reform. As I entered the registrar's office, I expected to see dusty files piled up to the ceiling. The files were there as expected, but right next to this pile were two newly installed computers with gleaming digital cameras to photograph the applicant as part of the process. I was expecting a speedy registry process but noticed that in fact the queues were longer than ever before. When I enquired about the reason for the delay, I was told that the files were being processed manually and then electronically. As it turned out, this was for the best, as halfway through the two-hour wait, there was 'load-shedding' – a wonderfully bureaucratic way of admitting that the power supply failed. The government needs to adopt transparent methods. But it is not enough to merely computerize the existing system. The root of the problem is that the process itself is too convoluted and needs simplification. Only then will the ordinary citizen get his or her due.

Our discussions kept us occupied as the train reached Vizag mid-afternoon. The welcoming party from the Eastern Naval Command was at the station and we were ushered into the naval auditorium for a briefing by Rear Admiral Ravi Chander Kochhar. He gave us a high-tech presentation on the challenges faced by his command. The laser light used by Admiral Kochhar traced India's vast seaboard contours on a large map as he described some of the strategic issues that India faced as a blue-water navy. The first Indian Navy aircraft carrier was commissioned as early as the 1960s. The Indian Navy is considered far ahead of other countries in this part of the world and its fleet may contain three aircraft carriers by 2010.

We were then treated to a visit to the submarines and destroyers that were anchored in the Vizag port. We met with the sailors and shared their experiences first-hand. We admired their fortitude and their ability to live at sea in confined quarters for long durations. As we mingled with the captain and his sailors, a different form of sacrifice and dedication came to light. The submarines in particular were seen as a dynamic fighting arm of the Navy. As we clambered through shoulder-width passages in these submarines, we admired the sailors' capacity to live for days within these confined quarters. Even the participants' second-class accommodation in the train seemed luxurious in comparison.

During the coming week, we were to travel across India to arrive back in Mumbai. We had circumnavigated most of the upper two-thirds of India and were to traverse the peninsula over the next week. We visited the beach at Vizag at night with the knowledge that a major leg of the journey was complete. Together, we walked towards the breaking surf as night advanced. Many participants had never been to a beach before. As the wind blew in from the Bay of Bengal bringing with it the tangy smell of salt air, we waded barefoot into the water to savour this eastern edge of India. These were moments of individual and group-bonding. We filled a jar with the sands of the Bay of Bengal with the intention of mixing the sand with a sample from the western shores of India.

10

Hyderabad Rising: An Enterprising South

Whoever looks for easy work, goes to bed very tired.

– YIDDISH PROVERB

Wednesday, 7 January 1998

From Vizag, we proceeded to Hyderabad. As the train approached the city, a giant statue of the Buddha rose from the waters of the Hussain Sagar Lake, which was built in the sixteenth century to help meet the city's water requirements. Hyderabad was also rapidly being noticed on India's economic map as a hub for enterprise. As we entered Hyderabad, we witnessed a transformation that is possible only when entrepreneurship takes root. The root cause of this transformation was the central theme of our discussion.

The Hyderabad we were visiting was in the process of transforming itself from a sleepy city, to a centre for rapid economic growth which was beginning to be compared to Bangalore. Hyderabad was starting to take the lead in IT, BPO, biotechnology and pharmaceutical industries. What was previously the headquarters of a largely rural and agricultural state was emerging as a centre for dynamic economic growth. We recognized that Chief Minister Chandrababu Naidu was responsible for this growth. He is a man of vision who adopted new methods to achieve greater results.

As part of the tour of Hyderabad, we visited the Golconda Fort and the Charminar. Around those ancient monuments was a city being reborn like no other we had encountered during our journey. Large highways were being built at breakneck speed. This had attracted companies like General Electric (GE) and Wipro to the city. Satyam Computers was founded in Hyderabad and has since then grown into one of the top four IT companies in India, standing on par with some of the best IT companies globally. Pharmaceutical companies such as Dr Reddy's Laboratories were also set up in Hyderabad.

Chandrababu Naidu took personal risks in ensuring that the state was run efficiently. His formula for rapid growth was a risky one to use in a rural state. His style of functioning was akin to that of a CEO of a large company. He surrounded himself with a team of builders, progressive bureaucrats and thinkers who were passionate about making a difference. He ensured that growth targets set by him were monitored by periodic conference calls which involved all district magistrates.

Chandrababu Naidu was also aware of the power of the outsider. He pulled out all stops to woo foreign investors. He was responsible for the relocation of the Indian School of Business to Hyderabad from Mumbai. When Jack Welch – the CEO of GE at the time – was to visit India, Naidu made sure that Hyderabad featured on his itinerary. He saw to it that his visit was planned with meticulous detail, to the extent of catering to his personal eating habits. The ability to attract external funding and more importantly, external know-how and talent was crucial to putting Hyderabad on the IT and bio-informatics map of India. Naidu holds the record of being the longest serving chief minister of Andhra Pradesh. His victory in the 1999 elections after a full term of rapid economic reforms was the first real indication that developmental politics was here to stay. This example is being followed in other states, and at least five chief ministers have fought and won elections in a similar manner.

An interesting story demonstrating Chandrababu Naidu's personal commitment to attracting outsiders to Andhra Pradesh was recounted by an acquaintance. A senior bureaucrat from Maharashtra had done exemplary work for the Municipal Corporation in accelerating urban development. He retired after a number of years of service. A few weeks after his retirement, he was relaxing at his home in Mumbai when the phone rang. The person on the other end said, 'Sir, this is Naidu speaking from Hyderabad. I want you to come to Hyderabad.' Flustered, the person wondered which Naidu this could be. The guttural voice at the other end intoned, 'Sir, this is Chandrababu Naidu, the CM of Andhra Pradesh. I am couriering two flight tickets for you and your wife, and I will be present at the airport to receive you day after tomorrow.'

With natural disbelief, the bureaucrat hung up, dismissing it as a crank call. A chief minister personally calling and speaking to a retired bureaucrat was unheard of. Sure enough, the next day the doorbell rang and he was presented with a letter from the CM's office with two air tickets to Hyderabad. When he reached

Hyderabad the next day with his wife, as promised Naidu was present to receive him at the airport. It was therefore no surprise that the retired bureaucrat took on the job offered to him. He relocated to Andhra Pradesh to head the urban planning and development projects for a number of years.

Was there something beyond the surface that allowed cities like Hyderabad and Bangalore to flourish? Was it just the genius and the energy of individuals like Chandrababu Naidu? Did important institutions such as Hindustan Aeronautics Ltd, Bharat Heavy Electricals and the Bio-informatics Institute in Hyderabad established by the government then become the platforms for growth and enterprise? But similar institutes had also been founded in the North by the government. The Central Drug Research Institute in Lucknow was one such example. Its presence, however, has not led to the emergence of any significant bio-medical companies. Was the climate in the South more conducive for outsiders to set up base? This may be true for Bangalore where from an early time the British, drawn by its salubrious environs, established clubs and administrative centres, but surely this was not a sustainable competitive advantage.

Our discussions returned to the basic foundation for entrepreneurship and progress – trust. It seemed to us that the atmosphere in the South was more self-assured. The North, though seemingly extrovert and confident, somehow had more conflict in interpersonal behaviour. In contrast, in the South there seemed to be an atmosphere of trust and cooperation.

Our discussions focused on the power of working together towards a larger goal. As a growing country, the ability to pull together towards a common goal is even more important than in a developed country. The ability to work as a group within and outside traditional family boundaries is a key ingredient for success. This is based on a feeling of mutual confidence which ensures that common goals are set and pursued while relying on others in the team.

Trust, according to the values group, was the foundation of every successful enterprise. They described trust as the 'branches' in the 'tree of perfection'. A sense of trust and integrity allows individuals to believe in others, it permits them to leave part of the overall building process to others and focus on their own contributions.

Our discussions also highlighted a perception that the North and South were starting to diverge. The South appeared to remain detached from the rest of the country and the North saw the South as politically unconcerned about the national agenda. The South had done more to promote education, especially with steps such as providing free lunch for all students. However, in demographic terms, the North is larger and growing much faster than the South. By 2025, it is expected that Bihar, Madhya Pradesh, Orissa, Rajasthan and Uttar Pradesh will make up nearly half of the country's estimated 1.3 billion population, and may contain 75 per cent of the country's poor.

On the train, we viewed things differently. The North often takes a lead in matters concerning politics. Our view was that the South has showcased how a strong economic order can be built. This creative tension and difference between the North and the South could spur both regions forward. For example, the concept of e-governance was spearheaded in Andhra Pradesh and Karnataka and has been adopted by Madhya Pradesh. And the private sector in Bangalore has realized that if the city's infrastructure is to improve, it needs to take a more active role and engage the political leadership as well.

The participants also discussed the importance of developing skills in relation to economic growth. The foundations of a successful enterprise are built by deploying skills in creating a product or a service that can be of use to others. Our system pays a lot of importance to general education and has ignored the development of skills necessary for enterprise and employment. Education is still largely shaped around passing examinations which is necessary but often insufficient in finding employment or earning a livelihood. The scarcity of talent faced by the IT and BPO industries in an ocean of graduates is one indication of this problem.

I noticed this particularly in eastern U.P., where an overdose of theoretical education and lack of skill-generating training has taken its toll. While visiting my village in Barpar, I often take long walks that lead me to adjoining villages. I have observed youngsters sitting on *charpoys* in the mango orchards that abut most village communities. In my interactions with these youngsters, I discovered that they had a Bachelor's and often a Master's degree in physics, history or psychology but remained unemployed. After receiving a traditional education, their first step was an examination to seek a job in the government. With the shrinking role of the state, these jobs are few and far between. Only a small number succeeds in passing these entrance examinations. After several attempts at clearing entrance tests, they return disheartened to the *charpoy* in the mango orchard. This results in a feeling of emotional and psychological failure. Once they see themselves as failures, their family and the village community also perceives them thus. This leads to a cycle of helplessness and a lack of confidence from which they are unable to recover. Since they consider themselves to be 'well qualified', these youngsters feel it below their dignity to help with farm work, and remain on the *charpoys* in the mango orchard.

My cousin, Bablu, managed to break out of this 'circle of unemployment'. After going through the process of sitting for various examinations, starting from the Indian Administrative Service to the local *munsifi*, he was a strong candidate to languish on the *charpoy* in the mango orchard. Then one day, Bablu decided instead to apply for an opening in a private company in Deoria. When he got a job as a salesperson, the village, unaccustomed to private sector jobs, smirked silently. But after a few years of hard work when he returned to the village one day as the regional sales leader with an air ticket for two for a sales conference in Bangkok, the village took note. Today, Bablu works hard, and when I meet him, I see him radiant and confident. Had he joined the local government, he would have pushed dusty files in the *tehsil* most of his life.

There is also another group of youngsters in these villages which has never had the opportunity for a proper education. Their parents are unable to put them through school, and they are forced to work to help till the soil from an early age. When the time comes for them to earn a livelihood, they leave the village to find work, usually as manual labourers in the bigger cities. Most find jobs in places like Mumbai, Delhi or Punjab working as migrant labourers. The lack of education, however, leaves them without the necessary skills to make a decent living. They rely on their physical strength as a means of livelihood. These unskilled workers are a source of income for the village. These youngsters who leave the village in search of a better living are often under-employed and their full potential is seldom recognized.

The India 2020 Vision Report by the Planning Commission uses homilies like 'employment must be considered a constitutional right of every citizen, backed by the full commitment of the government'. Making employment a constitutional right may be a pleasant sound-bite but on a more practical level, emphasis has to be placed on providing an atmosphere for generating the right skills.

If youngsters such as those from the mango orchard were instead trained in a particular skill, they would find better jobs. Given the right tools, the right training and with proper financial backing, they would be able to start companies, micro-enterprises and agro-industries. They would also provide other youngsters with much needed employment. The constraint lies in developing the necessary skills and a positive attitude towards entrepreneurship. Youngsters who migrate from villages in search of manual labour, could, given the right skills, find better paying jobs in the cities. I doubt if the migration from villages to cities can be stopped, nor should it be. However, if this exodus is slowed down by offering village youngsters job opportunities within the village, it will lessen the strain urban India is bound to suffer, not to mention the deprivation that results from young people leaving the village.

More important than an economic argument is a social one. Work on its own is liberating. While developed economies try to create leisure, in societies like India, lack of work itself is debilitating. It destroys self-confidence; it creates a culture of dissonance and friction. Work, on the other hand, creates a natural relationship between the individual and the system. And the individual feels connected and stretched. It is a well known fact that unemployment lurks in those areas in India where instability and terrorism are prevalent.

As more young people enter the workforce in the next twenty years India is going to undergo a sea change. I sometimes wonder if this will still be true if these young entrants to the workforce are unable to find work. If they come into the national mainstream without proper skills, will they be able to find employment? While the green revolution has taken us past the spectre of a food shortage, unemployment poses the next major challenge. The Indian economy, growing at 8 to 9 per cent per annum, is still not able to produce an increase in jobs that is required to keep pace with the 250 million more Indians who are expected to enter the workforce over the next twenty years. This is equivalent to adding the population of a country the size of England every five years to the Indian population. To cope with this growth, not only will we have to lead in the knowledge and service-based industries, we will also have to simultaneously accelerate agro-based industries and manufacturing industries.

If we are to get our demographic dividend, we have to motivate both the unemployed youths of the mango orchard as well as the youths who have left their villages in search of jobs to find employment-generative skills. Some, one hopes, will start agro-based businesses, thus creating more jobs. We will have to advertise the running of an enterprise as a positive calling. We may have to create a policy to provide protection in the form of insurance to some of them as they take risks in starting new businesses. We must, above all, protect them from the state, which in large parts of rural and mofussil India frowns on the creation of businesses and the generation of wealth, if one were to go by the rules and regulations that an entrepreneur has to navigate. We have to strengthen the state to regulate the country better as market forces emerge in smaller towns. This requires a more focused, stronger and better paid but smaller government. Unless the government plays a more friendly role, the country and these youngsters will not be able to achieve their potential.

A group of journalists from *Ananda Vikatan* were on the train with us. At each stop they sent a positive report back to their headquarters. We had unfortunately been unable to venture further south despite our intentions of doing so when we were planning the journey.

In the South, we had wanted to visit the Kalpakkam nuclear plant near Chennai, the emerging IT companies in Bangalore, a special industrial zone in Trivandrum, and the Rock Memorial in Kanyakumari. When this did not happen, the Tamil weekly made people in the region aware of our journey. *Ananda Vikatan* ran a seven-part series on the journey with photographs of the participants and a summary of the debates. The magazine's coverage of the *yatra* in the South exceeded our expectations. This was a small consolation as we left Hyderabad to complete the last leg of the journey.

Two individuals from the South were of enormous help in preparing for the *yatra* and their efforts had a strong impact on the project. Ashok Thomas ran a PR agency in Chennai and was introduced to me by Sandeep Reddy, a colleague from Accenture. When I arrived in Chennai to advertise the project, he put the full force of his agency, Adroit Consultancy, behind it. He took me to different parts of Chennai to drum up support from journalists, and organized a press conference to publicize the journey. It was largely because of Ashok's efforts that we managed to get a very strong contingent from the South which educated us about that part of the country.

During my visit to Chennai in preparation for the *yatra,* we scouted the IIT Chennai campus to see if a seminar could be hosted there. As Ashok's jeep drove us out of the IIT campus, I asked the driver to stop. A 5-foot wall separated us from the sea. Instinctively, Ashok and I jumped on the wall and surveyed the expanse of sea and the waves welling in from the east. As he looked at me, he must have seen my absorption in the scene, as though I was trying to grasp something of the underlying spirit of the South, in the same way that a visitor to the North would look at the Ganges at the Allahabad to try and get a sense of what it means to people in the North. I knew from previous visits to Chennai, that despite language differences, a number of people in the South were equally fascinated by my origins when I explained that my mother's ancestors were from Kashi.

The second person from the South who influenced the journey was Lieutenant General Sushil Pillai (retired), a friend of my father's and someone I look up to as a father figure. He has devoted his life to the Assam Regiment, and has written a history of the regiment. He had organized for us to visit local institutions in Thiruvananthapuram to showcase Kerala's achievements. While we did not make it that far south, his ideas and his passion for the project were a personal encouragement for me to continue with the journey.

Participants from the South like Durga, Mrinalini, Rakesh, Bharati and others brought with them a certain quiet dignity which impressed the other participants. It was no surprise then that most of the follow-up work was also organized in Chennai at the end of the *yatra,* led in part by Subhashish Sarkar. With Ashok Thomas's support, this group of nine-odd participants showcased their experiences in what they called the Level Crossing, a seminar attended by over 200 people. They talked to the audience about their experiences and aspirations. When participants recounted the journey individually they were usually met with disbelief similar to what we had experienced in the early days as organizers. But as a group aided by Ashok, the impact was comprehensive. Subhashish Sarkar, at that time a second-year student at IIT Chennai, also convinced its director to support future *yatras*.

While one of our bigger regrets is that we were unable to venture further south, the participation from that region more than made up for it during and after the *yatra.*

11

Aurangabad: Cultural Crosscurrents

Wisdom is a weapon of defence, an inner fortress no foe can raze.

– THIRUVALLUVAR

Thursday, 9 January 1998

From Hyderabad we left for Aurangabad, where we had planned a visit to the nearby Ajanta and Ellora caves. As we travelled the Deccan, the rugged landscape and craggy hills were a reminder of my own wanderings that had begun here. In class XI, with 500 rupees in my pocket, I had struck out alone southwards at the end of an athletic meet in Begumpet on the outskirts of Hyderabad. Rahul Sankrityayan was my inspiration at the time, and when the last class fellow backed out, I felt I could do it alone. I felt that this way I would be able to interact more closely with the people I met during the journey.

As I boarded the train for Bangalore in the general third class unreserved compartment, I found that a local goon had 'reserved' the only remaining upper berth. He wanted to charge an on-the-spot 'reservation fee'. I pretended to be part of a larger returning party of schoolboys and by pointing to the flash of hockey sticks they were carrying, I managed to occupy the berth without a single rupee being exchanged. I then spent an idyllic two weeks exploring the South. I slept in railway rest houses, and once on a park bench in the garden city of Mysore. Even then, as a youngster so many years ago, I had noticed the ease and warmth of the South, not to mention the efficiency of Vijaya Bank. So, when this Karnataka-based bank opened its branch in Lucknow, I was one of its first customers.

Our train pulled in at Aurangabad railway station, and we took buses arranged by TCI to visit the Ajanta and Ellora caves. Tucked away in the folds of a deep ravine of the Waghora river, the Ajanta caves were lost to the world for over 1200 years. They were rediscovered early in the nineteenth century and even today their beauty, grace and simplicity are startling. These second century caves took on a special meaning for the group. It was clear from looking at the ethereal cave paintings in Ajanta that they were a remarkable reflection of culturally evolved times. What makes them unique is the fact that kings were not the protagonists in the paintings. When kings were featured, they were usually in the background, proferring to support wise men, women or the lay public. It seemed that there were hints of a democratic gene even in those ancient times.

As we visited the caves of Ellora, we focused on the dominant Kailash temple, built in AD 765 and dedicated to Lord Shiva. These stunning rock excavations were completed in the course of a century. Over 175,000 metric tons of rock were excavated from the walls of the cliff to create the temple. As we stepped into this shrine, ancient Indian artistic talent exploded before our eyes. The motifs and figurines inside the temple gave an insight into the social milieu during the reign of the Rashtrakuta king, Krishna I.

The *dvarapalaks*, the gatekeepers of the temple, the goddesses Ganga and Yamuna, signifying purity and devotion, flanked the entranceway. A little further to the left was Vyas, the legendary author of the *Mahabharata*, and opposite him sat Valmiki, the poet-author of the *Ramayana*. On the other side of the inner door was the image of Kubera, the pot-bellied, jovial god of wealth. As we proceeded further into the temple, the familiar figure of Ganesa adorned the left wall, while on the right was Durga, slaying the demon Mahisa. Right in front of us was the Goddess Lakshmi, who presides over beauty, fortune and prosperity. Two sculpted panels of Shiva facing each other had Shiva in his different incarnations. On the right was Shiva as the lord of knowledge, *gyana dakshinamurti*, while on the left was Shiva as the energetic destroyer of evil. As we focused on *gyana dakshinamurti*, we noticed that Shiva of the four-armed *tandava*, had eight arms instead of four. Each of these eight arms sculpted 1200 years ago represented different forms of knowledge.

Frank and his cameras were in full motion in these picturesque surroundings. The camera captured the waterfall adjoining the cave structure, the dim lights of the main Ajanta caves, and the excitement of the participants. Frank's documentary showcased Purva as she travelled through India and in the process rediscovered herself. The documentary included her interactions with participants such as Devang Patel from the UK and Amita Kulkarni from Brown University, USA. The documentary also captured conversations between the Indian and international participants on the train.

To illustrate the international character of the participant profile, and with a canny eye on the international market, Frank assembled a diverse group in a compartment to film a debate that often took place spontaneously in the train. This particular group had Akhtar, Karthik, Hazel, Purva, Devang, Amita and Daniella, a participant from Mexico. Frank wanted to capture thoughts from across the international spectrum. After brief dialogues on a number of national and international issues, the topic turned to Kashmir. Akhtar stoutly defended the Indian policy on Kashmir, while Karthik suggested a more liberal approach to the issue. Hazel and Daniella watched from the sidelines, silenced for once. Frank also captured the natural buzz and energy on the train. He caught our contingent of ten deaf and dumb children on film dancing to the tune of the train's whistle. He filmed the catering staff cleaning utensils while singing folk songs. His camera captured the growing camaraderie on the train as we covered this third leg of the journey with Purva as his tired protagonist.

But after the *yatra,* Frank compensated Purva for all the hard work during the filming of the documentary. When Purva visited London a few years later, he took her for dinner to the British Academy of Film and Television Arts (BAFTA) club near Piccadilly Circus. He introduced her to eminent directors and actors as 'an upcoming actress from India'. Little did Frank realize that one of the people whom she was being introduced to was Saeed Jaffrey. As Saeed peered quizzically at this 'actress', Purva beat a hasty and well-timed retreat.

The India and the globe group led discussions on India's interaction with the world during our visit . We concluded that we have to adopt ideas from the outside world but adapt them to local conditions. Equally important is for us to make an effort to project our values and our culture to the outside world. This proactive approach is vital in a world where the two-hundred-year-old domination of industrial thinking is beginning to be questioned.

We discussed the relevance of some of the age-old value systems in India to the modern, post-industrial, knowledge and service economy. The concept of *guru-shishya*, the ideal of *nishkama karma*, the Sufi tradition of Islam may offer new insights to the modern world. A world entering the knowledge era can use them fruitfully. In fields as diverse as dress, habits, food and customs, India has a number of cultural and intellectual insights to offer the world.

The influence of western thought on the political, economic and cultural landscape of the world has been unprecedented over the last hundred years. Media presence and the proliferation of the Internet have accelerated this trend over the last three decades. As you go from one global village to another, from Mumbai to New York and London, cultural disparities are seemingly indistinguishable. Teenagers watch *The OC* in Delhi just as they do in Dallas. *Who Wants to Be a Millionaire* is popular in three continents. Young people wear similar clothes, and in all major Indian cities, a large number of people watch *ER* and 24.

Now a counter trend seems to be emerging. With over ninety years of filmmaking experience, Bollywood is beginning to produce films that are comparable to any in the world. These movies are popular in the Middle East, Nigeria, other parts of Africa, the Near East and parts of Russia. If you go to a Nigerian video store, you will find that the number of Hindi movies with English subtitles is surprisingly high. In Malaysia, the taxi-driver enquires instantly about Shah Rukh Khan. Way back in 1987, a young Yemeni lady ran away from home in search of Amitabh Bachchan.

In 2003, Bollywood exploded onto Oxford Street in London. Selfridges, an upmarket department store at the centre of London, organized a Bollywood month where its displays featured posters and memorabilia from Indian cinema. Classical Indian dances were also part of the experience. In the same year, the musical *Bombay Dreams* ran to a full house in London, although it was less successful in New York. This was not just because of the support of the large Indian community in London but because of the growing popularity of India. The story on the culinary front is even more exciting. It is well known that chicken tikka masala is UK's national dish. Most streets in the UK have an Indian or Bangladeshi restaurant. Some Indian restaurants like Benaras or Zaika are now considered mainstream.

The success of Deepak Chopra and Sri Sri Ravi Shankar and similar seers are examples of the growing acceptance of Indian thought and culture in the western world. While India has always had a mystical allure for the westerners who visited India in droves in the 1960s, India's economic success has made the world take notice. India appeals to diverse communities and nationalities be it a Nigerian, a Russian, the Yemeni lady or the British theatre-goer – all are able to relate to Indian culture.

In the UK, a number of second-generation Indians, who may not have even visited India, are also attracted to this culture. The *lehenga* and other accoutrements of Indian attire are far more visible these days on London streets than they were a few years ago. While their parents grew up with an element of embarrassment about India's poverty and sometimes about its garish culture, this new generation is flaunting their Indian heritage and getting a positive response from the rest of the world.

While travelling on the London Underground, one day, curiosity got the better of me. I noticed a young lady next to me carrying a sequined *jhola* which had photographs of Bollywood stars. It had a Hindi advertisement for 'Chutki' – a digestive made of betel leaves. I asked her what she found appealing about the bag. She said simply, 'I like it.' I detected a foreign accent and asked where she had purchased it from. I had an image of an east London shop in my mind. It turned out that she was an Italian student studying in London and had bought the *jhola* in Florence. A few stops later, as I was getting off the train, she tapped me on the shoulder and said, 'Can you tell me what it says?'

Indian culture is being projected with new-found energy. The refinement of Indian cinema, the excitement of Bhangra music, the talent and nuances of Indian classical dance forms, are all beginning to be appreciated across the world. The Indian government is also trying to promote tourism through its new advertising campaign, *Incredible India*. India appeals not only to nations who relate to Indian culture, but also to those who till recently were distant from it. Anokhi, Fabindia, BR films, Masala Zone have all found a market abroad. Much like the golden arches of McDonald's fast food, the roaring lion of MGM films and the popularity of Coke heralded the arrival of North American culture across the globe in the last century, we are beginning to see the gradual advance of Indian culture through these innocuous institutions.

However, before Indians declare victory, there is still a lot to be done at home. Most parents in India lament the fact that the youth fails to appreciate Indian culture and values. Young Indians, especially in large cities, are taking to western culture at a rapid pace. The answer, some suggest, to this problem lies in restricting access to the mass media, by controlling youngsters, and in making sure that their noses are pointed in the 'right' direction. This betrays a lazy approach to the issue. A more positive approach is to engage the minds and hearts of the young generation. India has to retain its core values and yet reinvent itself to appeal to the younger generation. The songs of Rabbi Shergill, the works of filmmakers such as Ram Gopal Verma and Ashutosh Gowarikar, are examples of such an approach. We have to do more than just revive ancient art forms. We have to make our cultural traditions relevant to today's world so that the modern generation is able to relate to them. The fault lies in the way we project our culture. We have been arrogant enough to assume that our youth will be proud of our heritage. The Society for Promotion of Indian Classical Music and Culture Amongst Youth (SPICMACAY) and other organizations have kept our culture alive in universities and schools. On the train, we discussed a need to fan their efforts by using our growing strengths in the mass media. This has started happening with a number of 'classical pop' genres and fusion music gaining a rapid following amongst young Indians.

This cultural exchange would benefit the rest of the world as well. In the vast flow of data and information across the globe, there is a strange paucity of new ideas. The current 'clash of ideas' between the Christian West and the Islamic world is shaping to be a negative engagement. Each sees the other as its nemesis. India, confident of its heritage and its capabilities, can provide a positive counterpoint. It can present an alternate world-view that seeks to push forward the stalled debate on new ideas. China with its ancient civilization, could also contribute to make this the Asian Age.

We came to the conclusion that economic and social enterprise was the answer to India's problems. But is there a cultural aversion to business and enterprise? And if this be the case, are there ways in which to solve this issue? In recent years, this has started to show in a schism between the private and the public sector. A number of political and economic commentators have remarked on the dichotomy between the public and private sectors in India. Bimal Jalan, former governor of the Reserve Bank of India, in his book *The Future of India* says: 'Economic renewal and positive growth impulses are occurring largely outside the public sector at the level of private corporations... autonomous institutions...or individuals at the top of their professions in India and abroad. In the government or public sector on the other hand, we see a marked deterioration at all levels...'

This is largely because 'good people are trapped in a bad system'. Most public servants start life wanting to serve their country. As their careers progress, realization dawns that their idealism and energy is feeding a machinery that has its own agenda. Those who try to reform it come up against vested interests of those who are directly benefitting from the system at the expense of the public. But this is under increasing scrutiny in a democracy where the average citizen is tired of remaining a supplicant. He is no longer solely reliant on the government as he has other service providers who serve him with honesty and efficiency. My visit to a phone company's service centre in Mumbai demonstrated this new face of customer service in India. The lady supervisor was busy but motivated and attended to each customer with a smile. The days of waiting at nationalized banks twiddling a brass token while in a long queue are over.

The communication revolution is rapidly changing the equation for the common man. Connectivity across the country is remarkable. From the small *rikshahwallah* to the helicopter-borne industrialist, everyone carries a mobile phone. According to Alvin and Heidi Toffler in *Creating a New Civilization* 'this change threatens the millions of mini bureaucrats whose sole source of power depends on their control of information fed up the reporting channel'. The Right to Information Act has also given ordinary citizens a conduit for truth. And slowly an economic culture has come to the fore, whether in the metros or in the towns and villages as the young join the workforce and seek opportunity.

In the world of politics, development and the resulting economic benefits to the electorate are beginning to be appreciated. While large numbers of voters are still illiterate, that has not prevented them from understanding which politician can best help develop their village or town. While caste divisions are still guiding factors, there is a new emphasis on the development vote. The politics of change, the politics of development – often overshadowed by the politics of division – are here to stay.

New ideas and energy are also filtering in from outside India. This is not just from Foreign Direct Investments (FDI) by the international multinationals alone, it is from the very genesis of our culture and national outlook. Today, Indian entrepreneurs are ready to take to new countries, ready to experiment, and are at ease with ambiguity. Infosys, Wipro, TCS, and now, Suzlon, Ranbaxy, and Tata Tea are but a few examples of the wealth created. In addition, there is a large NRI community consisting of fifteen to twenty million Indians with assets in the range of 40 to 60 billion dollars, not counting billionaires like Lakshmi Mittal. This includes a brain bank of doctors, engineers and lawyers who recognize that the opportunities in India are growing for them and their progeny. As natural adventurers who have ventured out in search of opportunities, they are perhaps more ready than others to take on the task of building India, provided they are given the right opportunities.

12

A Day in Ralegaon Siddhi: A Reformer in Action

If you don't practise, you don't deserve to dream.

– ANDRE AGASSI

From the Ellora caves, we proceeded to the Bajaj auto factory in Aurangabad. We wanted to spend time at the factory where Madhur Bajaj, a personal friend and well-wisher, had agreed to host a discussion at his main scooter plant. Madhur had been an early supporter of the *yatra*, coming as he does from a family who were keen supporters of Gandhi during the freedom movement. Gandhi considered Jamnalal Bajaj – the founder of Bajaj industries and Madhur's grandfather – to be his adoptive son. We wanted participants to interact with the management of the Bajaj auto factory and with Madhur personally, to hear how their family set up the scooter plant at Aurangabad. At the time, the plant was producing the largest number of two-wheelers in the world. The Bajaj auto business was making a transition from a family-run management structure to a professionally run company. It faced unprecedented competition from new entrants like Hero Honda and other manufacturers from Japan. The family faced up to this challenge and emerged successful because of their focus and passion for the scooter business. As we took a tour of the factory and saw gleaming scooters roll out from the assembly line, we understood the scale of the effort and depth of commitment that had gone into building this plant. It showed once again, the value of vision, sweat and toil.

We had agreed to present the results of the seven-point agenda to Madhur and his team at the end of this visit. These presentations in the sanctum of the Bajaj auto factory gave us a chance to conclude our discussions. The values group's 'tree of perfection' served well to structure their findings. The *azad nagar* group presented their findings in the form of a play. The scenes enacted showcased how a city with a number of social drawbacks could be transformed through their recommendations. The participants had been on the road for the last three weeks, and their presentations not only reflected their innermost thoughts, but an emotional involvement with their findings. Each group, at the end of their recommendations, proposed an action plan, and some also took a pledge to take matters forward.

Madhur was touched by these presentations and he in turn moved the participants by a speech which reflected the sentiments of his entire family. He had never imagined that one day a train would roll into his hometown to make this presentation. Madhur had sponsored five students from the Nath Valley School to take part in the journey, and as our discussions concluded, each of them came forward to thank him personally.

Madhur asked me to attend a dinner organized at the Bajaj auto factory that evening. Rahul Bajaj, his elder brother and the head of the family, was also going to be present. He asked me to come to his home before the event, where he introduced me to his extended family. What struck me about the Bajaj clan was their simplicity despite being one of the most prosperous families in the country. The Jamnalal Bajaj legacy seeks to build large companies while helping the communities which contribute to the growth of the companies. Once, on a bus journey from Mumbai to Shirdi, I had sat next to a peon who had worked in the Bajaj factory all his life. His description of the family and their attitude towards workers confirmed my views that the Bajaj philosophy ensured the prosperity of both the company and society. Madhur spent the evening with the participants on the train. His support for the journey was immense and his visit inspired a number of participants.

The Nath Valley School nearby also arranged a welcome for us. The welcome was led by its principal, Ranjit Dass, who had been involved with the school from its inception. The school had been founded with help from Madhur and others in the Aurangabad region with the aim of giving students a twenty-first century education. The students organized a special reception. The highlight was a multi-cultural dance, combining music from the East and the West and concluding with Rahman's ubiquitious *Vande Mataram*. The dancers' hands were painted with the colours of the national flag and there was a sense of energy about the celebrations that inspired us. The five participants from Nath Valley who had taken part in the journey were given special importance that day. But Ranjit Dass also gently challenged us on the seven-point agenda. As a passionate educationist, he felt that education should have been given its share of importance. The group in charge of organizing the next *yatra* at this point took note.

In Aurangabad, an incident that took place posed a challenge to me personally. During the course of the journey, we had changed the route to enable us to stop in Pune. This sudden change in route involved re-ticketing with possible additional expense. I was at a loss, as I did not know how to raise these additional funds at short notice. I requested a number of sponsors for a loan but when this did not yield results, the only solution was to go to the stationmaster at Aurangabad and request him to delay the transaction till we reached Mumbai. Actually, the railways owed us money, as we had overpaid at the initial point of payment. I could not share my concerns with other organizers or *yatris* lest it dishearten them. Instead, I walked up to the stationmaster with a rehearsed pitch to get him to agree to delay the ticketing process. Before I could speak, he said that he was not in a position to accept payment in Aurangabad. He advised me to settle the matter with Western Railway once we reached Mumbai. Immediately, the load I was carrying lifted. I changed the itinerary and walked back to the train with the new tickets in hand. As on numerous other occasions while organizing the event, it felt as if someone up there was watching over us.

The stories of the two blind participants are a remarkable reflection of their fortitude and enterprise. Radheyshyam is the blind son of a bricklayer in Madhya Pradesh. When his drunk father took to beating him and his siblings, he was adopted as a young child by a school for blind children. Radheyshyam was sixteen years old, he did not speak a word of English and travelled for two days alone on a train from Jabalpur, to arrive at the IIT Mumbai convocation hall to take part in the journey. For the first week, he was a somewhat silent spectator since he did not have an urban pedigree. Now that the group had started to gel together, his latent talents came forth in bursts of Hindi poetry.

Akhtar, also blind, came from Assam and was adopted by a cleric and thereafter made his way to a blind school in Mumbai. He had often interjected our discussions with some of the most probing questions. He also led the discussions around the seven-point agenda. Akhtar initially came across as a bright, soft-spoken youngster. He studied in an English-medium school in Mumbai and spoke fluent English. In Amritsar, prior to the *bhangra* performance at the school soon after our visit to the Golden Temple, we requested him to say a few words to the guests. As he took the mike, the participants expected to hear the slightly clipped English tones of Akhtar. Instead, he delivered a ten-minute extempore speech in chaste Hindi as participants and organizers gawked at this demonstration of his linguistic skills.

Radheyshyam and Akhtar were opposites in nature but symbolized some of the contrasts present amongst our group. Both were silently discovering an India we saw in resplendent colours. Akhtar had the ability to dissect an argument and then piece it together, while Radheyshyam, with his boundless optimism, was keen to create an India full of the colours of his poetry. They often saw India more clearly than us.

But Akhtar's story did not end there. It ended tragically five years later when Akhtar took his own life in the blind school of which he was such a proud student. Akhtar was the ideal participant. He was idealistic, came from an urban school, but had spent his early days in a small-town environment in Assam. His English was so perfect that Devang called him 'Lord Akhtar'. And yet, as we discovered in Amritsar, Akhtar's Hindi could put a U.P. wallah like me to shame. Then why this tragic end?

Devang, who was a few years older than him, related an incident which occurred during the discussion at the Bajaj auto factory which demonstrated Akhtar's presence of mind. When Devang was put on the spot by one of the facilitators to ask Madhur a question, he turned instinctively to Akhtar. Within seconds, Akhtar composed a meaningful question which got Devang out of an awkward spot. Akhtar never asked for help and like Radheyshyam, he had a fresh perspective on any topic of discussion.

After the *yatra*, Devang visited him at his blind school on a couple of occasions as he had struck up a friendship with 'Lord Akhtar'. Devang could not help remarking how Akhtar, who appeared so normal except for his impared vision, was so totally out of place in a disabled school. Perhaps there was a hidden message in Akhtar's passing. Akhtar did not want pity or help; he wanted to be treated as a mature adult. He had demonstrated this amply during the course of the journey. He never asked for help, and more than once offered to help others on the train. During our discussions, he had railed at the stigma of India being termed as a 'poor nation'. Akhtar believed that we were different, poor in a number of areas where we had to improve, but rich in many other areas – very much like Akhtar himself. Perhaps when Akhtar was unable to get this point across to society, one day, he decided to leave.

Sunday, 12 January 1998

The next day we departed for Ahmednagar, where the Armoured Corps Centre and School had organized a reception. Major General J.S. Varma, a family friend, was commanding the Armoured Corps Centre and School, and had arranged for a reception in the mess hall of the centre as well as a tank ride for the participants. Surrounded by a group of *yatris* in the trophy-lined mess hall, he gave an impromptu speech on the Armoured Corps and its purpose. The Armoured Corps have defended the Indian borders twice since independence. This experience, similar to that with the Navy in Vizag, gave participants an insight into the importance of the defence forces in the life of the nation. Major General Varma had been with the 63rd Cavalry which had also been my father's regiment. Visiting him and my childhood town was a much needed break for me.

I had lived in Ahmednagar for three years when my father was a colonel in the Army. My sister and I have many happy memories of our large house in the cantonment, where we spent innumerable afternoons by the tamarind tree, and by the stream next to our house which would overflow during the monsoons. We spent the best days of our childhood there, watching movies and devouring Jim Corbett's and Kenneth Anderson's books on Indian wildlife. Some of my best student days were in Kendriya Vidyalaya. Straight from Delhi, we found the school in contrast to be a paragon of egalitarianism. We studied, fought and played with the poorest to the richest children in town. I learnt Marathi songs, hid in the moat of the Ahmednagar fort looking for jackfruit, visited the monument, Chand Bibi Ka Maqbara, in the nearby hills and learnt early in life that India was more than the annexe at the army club.

As the participants were being introduced to the Armoured Corps on this visit, I took the opportunity to visit our old house, surprising the brigadier and his family with my misty-eyed passion in exploring the old bungalow.

~

From Ahmednagar, we proceeded to a village that has been recognized across India as an example of commitment to a rural cause. This visit to Ralegaon Siddhi would also be a testing ground to see whether some of the ideas on our seven-point agenda were relevant in a rural environment. Anna Hazare, a modern-day Gandhi, had done exemplary work in Ralegaon Siddhi for rural and social upliftment. Single-handedly, he had changed the lives of villagers in Ralegaon Siddhi and the adjoining areas, and the village is an example of innovative rural development for the rest of the country.

Anna was there to greet us when we arrived. Diminutive in height, Anna towers with passion when he speaks of village development. He had a busy schedule but was intrigued by the concept of our *yatra*. We were equally curious about this famous personality.

Anna's early career was that of a subedar in the Indian Army. In an encounter in the 1965 war, his battalion had been wiped out. He was driving an army truck, and by a miraculous turn of fate, escaped unharmed. As he was travelling back from the war front to his village in Ralegaon Siddhi, he chanced upon a book by Swami Vivekananda. Reading this book after his brush with death made him realize that his life had a higher mission. If he was the only survivor in a battalion where everyone else had been killed, he had a divine debt to repay. As he returned to his village, he was struck by its poverty and lack of development. There was a lack of infrastructure in the village, alcoholism was rampant, water was scarce, illiteracy was pervasive, and women were treated very poorly. Agriculture, which was the mainstay of the village and adjoining areas, was poorly managed and as a result, there were very few villagers who wanted to stay in the village.

Anna is renowned for his hard work and a tough, no-nonsense manner, but he is also an astute judge of how to bring about change. Instead of starting by pointing out these various social and economic ills to the villagers, Anna brought the villagers together to work towards a non-divisive common goal. He chose to build a temple which gained the support of the whole village. He got individuals and families to give a hand, and once the temple was built, he started motivating them for other common tasks. He formed his own five-point agenda for village development which had practical themes like water conservation, fight against alcoholism, and similar issues that would improve the quality of life for the villagers. He also worked hard at nurturing and educating students in the village and making them aware of the social issues surrounding them.

It took time but over a period of ten years social and economic changes started to become visible. He astutely showcased these advances to motivate the villagers further so they could understand the worth of their hard work and achievements. He used visual aids to point out the distinct change in the village with 'before and after' photographs. The contrast and obvious prosperity and resulting pride were palpable in Ralegaon Siddhi.

Anna personally took us around his village to show us geodesic domes – the structure created by Buckminster Fuller which provided a model for inexpensive housing that could be created by local artisans. He also pointed out how by creating bunds water drainage could be controlled and over time the water table could be raised. He took us to his schools which had some of the most impressive IT and computer equipment I had seen until then in rural India.

Frank and his camera crew were keen to film Anna in this rural setting. Frank asked me to walk with Anna as he explained the benefits of these domes. Perched on the roof of a nearby house, Frank had his crew train their cameras on us as we walked down a flight of steps. But Frank had forgotten Anna's name. After waving his arms in an effort to attract Anna's attention, Frank finally hollered in frustration, 'Can you ask the "great man" to look up to his right?' We burst out laughing, and Anna willingly complied.

Anna leads by example. We saw him sleep late at night, rise as early as 5 a.m. and devote much of his waking hours to pursuing his vision single-mindedly. If required, he did not shy away from enforcing discipline. At a time when he was fighting rampant alcoholism in the village, a few erring young men were summarily punished by Anna and his team. Some thought that he was being unduly harsh but his methods, such as those based on his service training, and his hands-on approach, were proving to be successful.

In recent times, Anna has locked horns with a number of political parties ever since he launched a single-handed action plan against corrupt government officials. He has also been a central force behind the right to information crusade. Some have also said that he harbours political ambitions. Our view was that with the dedication and integrity he has shown in creating Ralegaon Siddhi, not only does he deserve to be a prominent public figure, other politicians should be following his example.

In the latter part of the journey and in my various discussions with the *yatris* after our travels had concluded, they often remarked that the visit to Ralegaon Siddhi was one of the greatest learning experiences of the *yatra.* The timing was right as we had digested our own thoughts by then. The seven-point agenda had been discussed and we had seen some of our ideas being implemented by Anna Hazare. Being with Anna for over twenty-four hours had given us an opportunity to see a practitioner in action. More importantly, Anna's grassroot approach, and the clarity of his mission helped us understand that dreams alone are not enough, that only consistent long-term action brings about positive change. But Anna Hazare and Bunker Roy also introduced the participants to a different side of India. They introduced us to the reality and urgent need of developing rural India, far removed from the IT-led India being applauded internationally.

As night fell, we slept on the floor in one of the large halls that Anna had created for visitors like us. That night, the boys got together and entertained each other with old Kishore Kumar songs. We slept late and got up early, following the example of Anna. When we woke up, it was still dark and somewhat chilly, but in the growing light, we could see a mass of students participating in drills at the school playground. The regimen for the children was tough; the hour was early, but the sheer energy of the village, especially its youngsters, was infectious. As we walked up to the hills adjoining the village to watch the sunrise, the realization dawned that we had come to the end of our journey.

All through the journey, we had asked various dignitaries and luminaries as to what the mission of young India should be. We recognized that the clarity of purpose provided by the struggle for independence was different as compared to tackling the problems of India today. If that was an idealistic sprint, this was a purposeful marathon which required a clearer direction. The force and clarity with which Anna Hazare's actions spoke gave us the answer we had been searching for. Anna said that our mission should be to create an India which was economically strong. An India where we were more developed, better fed, better clothed and with more opportunities for ourselves and our children; an India where Indians put personal matters of religion, caste and class aside; a developed country with its own ethos and imprint. Anna echoed our sentiments by invoking the soil he so dearly loved. He said, 'One grain has to bury itself alive to give birth to a field of crops. By burying itself, the grain does not die. India today needs people like that grain.' This was the India we had been envisioning over the last three weeks and that is what we saw being created right before our eyes at Ralegaon Siddhi.

As we boarded the train after this overnight stay at Ralegaon Siddhi, the common sentiment among the participants was one of re-affirmation. Our thoughts had been implemented here. Anna had spent significant time with the *yatris*, and was a source of inspiration to all of us. As we left Ralegaon Siddhi, we knew that the journey was now coming to its physical and intellectual conclusion.

13

Journey's End: Thoughts on the Next Yatra

The real voyage of discovery consists not in seeking new landscapes, but in having new eyes.

– MARCEL PROUST

Monday, 13 January 1998

From Aurangabad we left for Pune, the centre of the Maharashtrian renaissance. A number of national leaders like Bal Gangadhar Tilak and Gopal Krishna Gokhale came from this city. This was also the birthplace of Dr Dhondo Keshava Karve, who has done remarkable work for the emancipation of women in modern India, including coming up with the idea of giving free education to the women in Maharashtra. He established a number of educational institutions for women in Maharashtra, making others around him understand the simple truth that progress in a society has to be preceded by the progress of women.

It was encouraging to see a large number of women participating in the *yatra*. Not only did they show up in large numbers – almost

45 per cent of the participants consisted of women – they took an active role in the discussions, debates and the organization of the journey. Durga, Gitanjali, Juhi, Neha, Komal, Purva and others were seen as natural leaders during the course of the journey. They shouldered their responsibilities and came up with creative – often contrarian – suggestions and were central in creating the Manifesto of Young India. This was a welcome and pleasant surprise given the fact that women are not encouraged to travel on their own in India.

It occurred to me that women's participation in the journey and their influence in India's future was significant in the country's development. Both Gauri and I dream of an India where our daughters Tarini and Isha, and others of their generation, will find an atmosphere which will enable them to realize their full potential. Tarini, who was in her mother's womb when these debates were taking place, will always have an Abhimanyu-like attraction towards the *yatra*. Isha, who came into this world four years later, was promptly named after the goddess of strength.

The sacred feminine has always had special significance in Indian philosophy. But to frame what I mean by the sacred feminine involves describing it in a language which has its own interpretation of the term. For me, the feminine represents creative energy. In Vedantic thought, the universe is embodied in *brahman*, whose still centre is the male principle, *shivam*, and the dynamic energy is the female principle, *shakti*. These two distinct qualities are interdependent and share equal status. The female represents the manifestation of creative energy or power. The two are similar to the yin and yang of far eastern culture; *shakti*, the yin, is an equal partner to *shivam*, the yang. Most images of power and energy in Indian culture still retain their feminine form. This offers a new definition of courage – a courage defined not by bravado but by resoluteness.

An analysis of the role of women in Indian mythology and history demonstrates that they were looked upon as equal pillars of society. Ancient texts and mythological stories talk of the woman first, then the man. A number of ancient women philosophers like Gargi were powerful and knowledgeable sources of thought and wisdom. Ashoka's daughter, Sanghamitra, played a bigger role in spreading Buddhism than her brothers. Closer in time, tales of Jijabai, Rani of Jhansi, Razia Sultan, Ahilyabai, Chand Bibi, not to mention the large number of women involved in the freedom struggle, are examples of the importance of women's role in Indian society.

Women have outdone men in numerous fields. In the world of enterprise, they are seen as the more reliable creditors as demonstrated by the NGO SEWA and by the Grameen Bank. They work better in a group, and help create sustainable means of livelihood. However, 300 years of an industrial, masculine framework continues to frame our thinking and our actions in a way that disturbs this balance. India can help restore this balance as it defines its own principles for development.

Even in the West, the emergence of women political leaders – Angela Merkel in Germany, Hillary Clinton and Condoleezza Rice in the US, and more recently Ségolène Royal in France – has led commentators to remark on the growing feminization of society. Jacques Seguela, a commentator on French politics, says, 'Virile values have prevailed in previous centuries: courage, power, strength, competition, domination. But over the past twenty years, feminine values have become more important: tenacity, harmony, balance, listening, tolerance, generosity.'

As the knowledge and the service economies continue to take the lead, the talent of women has to be brought centre stage in India. Instead of going to a field to till the soil, or to a factory to tighten a bolt with a wrench, women put their minds to good use. In this area women can be far more talented. The sustainable development movement has a direct link with women. In India, the earth is popularly considered as a mother. The Bishnoi sect in Rajasthan sees preservation of the environment, its flora and fauna as a natural process of respecting the mother. The Jains are similarly influenced in their approach to life. Instead of looking at nature as a source of raw material to feed an industrial machine, we on the train discussed how we could use the creative power of women to work with the environment.

Our approach was different from that adopted by a number of Indian environmentalists who say that economic growth is harmful to the environment. These are Luddites and lazy environmentalists. They remain cocooned in a make-believe world where material progress is not considered important. Our discussions comprehensively rejected this stance. Our view was that growth, progress and engagement in the material and physical world is important. But it had to be done keeping a sustainable approach which can be provided by women in Indian society.

The ground reality, however, is very different. Women are treated very poorly in India, often exploited by a male-dominated society. In India, women still have poor economic and social standing, and remain second-class citizens. In rural India, the situation is particularly alarming. Child marriages still abound, and a significant number of Indian women remain behind the veil. From a very early age society instils a sense of inferiority in them. Clearly, a number of women have risen to the top in the subcontinent, but they have done so against enormous odds. Though our *yatra* had a far greater participation from women than we had anticipated, even we noticed signs of women's oppression as we travelled across the country.

A woman-led environmentally friendly, sensitive, creative and nurturing ideology can be easily construed by other civilizations as a call for a submissive India, embracing the 'phantom of pacifism', a temptation for aggressive nations and therefore a positive danger to peace. A balanced India is not a submissive India. And that is how it should be in any healthy society. This was best expressed by the famous modern Hindi poet, Maithilisharan Gupt, to the effect that, 'Forgiveness can only adorn the snake which has venom.'

The famous historian-philosopher Fernand Braudel, in his book *A History of Civilizations,* talks of India as 'the Cinderella civilization, beautiful, gifted, destined for greatness but relegated to the backstage by those domineering sisters of Islam and Christendom'. Now that Islam and Christianity are engaged in a cultural war that has taken an alarming turn, India has to come forward to provide an ideological counterpoint.

The anthropologist Claude Lévi-Strauss defines the ascent of man as the journey from nature to culture in its ability to live with an otherness. Otherness refers to a society that is open to other points of view while holding onto its own ideas. India, in particular, defines this in its philosophy as the balance between the male and the female. During the course of the journey, we had reconciled the differences between the PLUs and PLTs, the difference between the North and the South, the difference between international and national perspectives. In our discussions during the seminar at IIT Delhi, we had reconciled an eastern intuitive vocabulary with western scientific thought.

The Hindi poet Jaishankar Prasad expresses this duality as the secret gift of nature: '*Dukh ki pichli rajani beet, prath ka hua naval prabhat/ ise mat jao tum kabhi bhool, iska yah rahasya vardaan.*' 'Do not forget the dark night which has passed because only that defines and makes the bright morning radiant.' We felt that the success of the Indian nation and its democratic experience is deeply rooted in its willingness to live with varying points of view.

As the Internet, mass media, mobile communications make rapid inroads into our lives, another form of divide is starting to occur and will take up momentum in the future. Ben Macintyre, a columnist for the *Times*, says, 'On the one side is the young culture of Internet – anarchic, playful, joyful, often inaccurate, increasingly global and uncontrollable; on the other, a paper-based set of priorities – precise, polite, and often national in perspective.' I saw this during the celebrations in Parliament on India's fiftieth year of independence, and we saw it on the train as a contrast between the PLUs and PLTs. As one gains momentum, the other will still exist. Instead of moping about this digital divide, India is well-equipped to reconcile these two worlds in the twenty-first century.

But this 'otherness' also has an implication for the developmental path we choose for India. The ability to absorb different points of view while holding onto our beliefs allows us to think, behave and live differently from the 'successful' West; it also makes us uniquely qualified to present a different world-view. Non-Indians have an important role to play in this process. As Indians start understanding and interacting with other cultures in growing numbers, other cultures must also understand and give space to India and its diverse customs. If I touch my father's feet and pay more respect to elders in general, that is part of my inheritance. The banyan tree is very different from the olive tree, but both provide a similar intellectual shade to their respective cultures.

Tuesday, 14 January 1998

As the train reached Pune, we recognized that the end of the journey was near. Karthik, Komal, Clyde and others were working frenetically on compiling the manifesto.

In Pune, we visited an NGO, Green Thumb. In the lush environs of Colonel Patil's aesthetically decorated house, the team took turns to plant saplings under the name of *Azad Bharat Rail Yatra*. One day we hoped to return to this city to find these saplings grown into blossoming trees.

As the train started winding its way back to Mumbai down the Western Ghats, our thoughts turned to the future. The *yatri* group came up with a proposal for sustaining this event in the years to come. As organizers, we had initially intended the *yatra* to be a one-off event, but the *yatri* group wanted to create a framework for the next expedition. As we discussed this in the common room, Akhtar voiced an important question which had been on our minds for some time, 'Are we going to be a Columbus in these *yatras*, going out to seek new frontiers? Or will we be more like Thomas Edison, creating something which will provide durable value?'

The general consensus was to use the *yatra* as a platform to engage young Indians on a voyage of discovery. This was to be as much a discovery of India as it was a personal discovery of one's aims, life goals and aspirations in the company of like-minded youngsters of a similar age. We recognized that the obvious benefit from a venture such as this was the process of learning as a group and its positive message of change. On a personal level, this 'life-changing' event had the potential to give direction when direction was most needed. We also wanted to set ourselves apart from a number of institutions and NGOs in India who were also doing development work. Our aim was to be different and in doing so add to the efforts of others.

We want the next *yatra* to focus on the South and the East. It will include mainly places like Tilonia and Ralegaon Siddhi, and perhaps not so many of the historical locations we had visited on the first *yatra*. It will involve lengthier stops. We also want more participants to take part, and we want to organize the journey at a time when there are less chances of fog. We want greater interaction from the local people we will meet during our travels.

The core *yatri* group has been brainstorming for the next *yatra*. Our motto is 'awakening entrepreneurship' by creating an annual 'semester on wheels'. We hope to address issues of employment and encourage economic activity by showcasing successful enterprises in the country. But we cannot restrict ourselves to mere economic enterprise. As a young country where markets will still take time to mature, especially in smaller towns and villages of India, we want to highlight social entrepreneurs like Bunker Roy, Ila Bhatt, Anna Hazare and others. Our research has thrown up a number of such institutions in India which are doing ground-breaking work in social development. The next *yatra* plans to visit such institutions. They may not be profit-seeking organizations but they are sustainable. They may not be as well known as Tilonia or Ralegaon Siddhi but silently they keep our foundation strong.

The next *yatra* will focus on such economic and social enterprises. Future *yatris* will try to understand the trials and joys of creating and nurturing something that benefits the entrepreneur and society as it forces change, pushes and applauds building. We plan to re-visit Tilonia, Ralegaon Siddhi, the Green Thumb in Pune and other locations to see if the saplings we planted nine years ago have taken root. We also plan to revisit SEWA, Grameen Foundation, Amul, Infosys and others. These institutions have demonstrated a model that has been the engine of India's growth. The individuals behind these successful institutions are the heroes who have focused their life's energies on creating something bigger than themselves. These Level 5 institutions and individuals will continue to build the India of the future.

At this time, we may have our own Level 5 leader in A.P.J. Abdul Kalam. He is not a Level 5 leader because he lived in a two-bedroom flat in Delhi before he moved into the Rashtrapati Bhavan. He is not a Level 5 leader because he came to important meetings in bush shirts and had to borrow clothes to attend formal occasions. He is not a Level 5 leader for his unassuming style, although it is important in his role as a national leader. He is a Level 5 leader because at various stages of his career, he thought of the long-term solution instead of seeking a quick fix. He is a Level 5 leader because he worked for a goal bigger than himself, in his case building ISRO and the Defence Research and Development Organization (DRDO). He is a Level 5 leader because he has been uncompromising in his quest for excellence.

There are other Level 5 leaders in our country, and they have all focused their efforts on building something larger than themselves. An institution which grows beyond the identity of the person creating it is what truly helps a society to develop. Narayan Murthy has done it at Infosys where for over fifteen years he and his team focused on building the company. In the current growth euphoria where Infosys has crossed the two-billion dollar figure, we often ignore the fact that it took Infosys fifteen years to reach a hundred-million-dollar revenue mark. Anna Hazare's crusade in Ralegaon Siddhi for rural development is also an example of a Level 5 leader. My father, instead of playing golf in the cosy suburbs of Noida after retiring from the Army, left the three-star comforts of his staff car and took to the bumpy U.P. state transport buses to serve his district in eastern U.P. My guru and teacher, Dr P.L. Dhar, has dedicated his life to building young minds in IIT Delhi. There are scores of others who are still doing this at this very moment but who go largely unrecognized. Two factors conspire against them. First, good news does not make good print. Second, their effort takes time to show results, especially in a nation of a billion humans beings. Our society looks for instant silver bullets.

During the next *yatra*, we want to have an open-ended discussion that gives young Indians positive exposure rather than forcing them down a particular path. By visiting institutions and promoting entrepreneurship, we hope to highlight what is already a growing groundswell of enterprise in the country. We want to address a central issue that Susan Davis of the Ashoka Foundation highlighted when talking of social entrepreneurship: 'One of the most difficult challenges is overcoming widespread scepticism. In the midst of media that is overwhelmingly tragedy-and-conflict-oriented, it is very rare to showcase constructive people who are optimistic and exude a positive energy.'

But the press only creates news that we like to read. Unless we start looking for positive stories, we will not break this negative cycle. We hope that future *yatras* will help catalyse this process.

In order to make a difference, not just individuals, not just the government, but a group of individuals have to come together to create institutions. The result will be institutions imbued with the collective energy and passion of that group. But in cases where markets are still shallow, they have to be driven by a cause that is wider than mere economic production of goods and services. Micro-finance is one such mechanism where social equity creates the basis for a group to come together so that sustainable enterprises can be created.

We also want more involvement from the Indian diaspora in the next *yatra*. Youngsters from across the globe are often curious about this growing country. They often read of India and China in the same breath, and have a new-found empathy for India that goes beyond just an affinity for the homeland. They see in this story of growth an opportunity to exercise their own entrepreneurial skills.

Recently, Gitanjali's husband, Kaustav Bhattacharya, who was born and brought up in the UK, has become excited about the next *yatra*. He sees in India a fresh platform on which to exercise his entrepreneurial aspirations. Kaustav currently works in London, but India appeals to him on a cultural – and increasingly – economic level. The concept of the *yatra* will appeal to people of Indian origin like Kaustav.

A number of young Indians who are studying or working abroad will naturally want to contribute. The story of India is an exciting one. New intellectual and emotional frontiers have to be conquered. New systems and institutions have to be built. There is adventure in the air. In contrast, some of the more developed economies like North America and Europe have already built those systems. The India story should, and must, attract adventurers back to India. This attraction for the homeland has inspired other non-residents to help serve their country. As described by Thomas Friedman in his path-breaking book *The Lexus and the Olive Tree,* the need to identify is as important as the need for material wealth. Indians abroad, often seen driving the ubiquitous Mercedes-Benz, still identify with their 'banyan tree'. India is still perceived as an ancient culture. But in the world of tomorrow, it can also be identified with a progressive and prosperous democracy, welcoming back its wanderers or *ghumakkads*.

The task of building the largest democracy in the world requires talent from across the world. If Adnan Sami has chosen Mumbai over Karachi for his musical talents, or if Mark Tully has adopted India, then we need others like them. Our ability to attract the talented, the visionary and the adventurous from other parts of the world will be the key to success. They will bring a certain rationality to balance the passion of Indians. This was a role the NRIs and the non-Indian contingent played in the *yatra*, and this role can be taken up by other talented migrants to India.

The growth of India over the next fifty years will mirror the growth that took place in North America over the last 200 years. An evocative book that captures this change is the Pulitzer Prize winning effort of Daniel J. Boorstin – *The Americans: The Democratic Experience.* The author traces the creation of myriad institutions in North America as it grew from a former colony of the British to the pre-eminent economic and social model of the last century. This story's context is starkly different from that of India. But the analogy is helpful: institutions were created in a country which had a different geographic, demographic, intellectual and emotional setting from Europe. The USA had a strong European intellectual influence to start with, but the reason it succeeded is because it adapted that mindset to suit its own environment. They created a national university system which moved learning beyond the Ivy League colleges. The Americans perfected an insurance network, they created a food distribution system where meat became the common man's food. They invented an aerospace industry where beginning with Pan Am, they broke new grounds in aviation. India will have to create similar institutions and systems over the next fifty years.

However, as North America became a successful industrial nation powered by oil, Model T cars and the threads of Amtrak that started criss-crossing its vast landmass, Boorstin warned of the dangers in blindly following existing, 'successful' models and the 'momentum' they generate. 'Fewer decisions of social policy seemed to be Whether-or-Not as more became decisions of How-Fast-and-When.'

As globalization has made the world a smaller place, a number of emerging countries like India run the risk of not asking Whether-or-Not questions. As India starts accelerating forward in its own 'democratic experience', we have to be careful of not heading down the How-Fast-and-When tunnel. At the start of its own journey, North America borrowed its intellectual heritage from Europe, but moulded it to the reality of North America, and we face a similar challenge at this juncture.

As early as the American Revolution in the eighteenth century, Benjamin Franklin declared his bubbling ambitions for the USA: 'The cause of America is the cause of all mankind.' Dean Acheson, the great American statesman and lawyer, called America 'the locomotive at the head of mankind'. But Acheson's colourful vocabulary also speaks of an industrial heritage. America dominated the twentieth century with its engineering skills, perhaps best represented by the word 'locomotive'. Its beliefs were shaped by the massive expansion of technology across its vast landmass over the last century.

When Gandhi, Tagore and Vivekananda talked of a universal Indian culture, they were as energetic and perhaps as arrogant as Franklin. But their instinct was to draw from our intellectual heritage which has always revered knowledge. The ideas themselves may not be modern, but the ability of a nation to accept different ideas like the electronic village may be where our genius lies. True success for us will be measured in our ability to create a world where service and knowledge are the new locomotives of growth. We have to create a path by asking Whether-or-Not questions of the development path laid down by the industrial West.

What we must adopt from the West is the spirit of scientific enquiry. But the age of networks, electrons, biotechnology, agri-business and the relevance of intangible assets must warn us against creating mechanical institutions. As this is the beginning of our own journey of development, we can use and connect with the Indian mind which has always respected knowledge and respects service.

The new environmental awareness that has spread across the developed world is asking fundamental questions about lifestyles and the cost of progress in the West. Commentators have declared that the 'demand for a carbon-free power is about to become the most disruptive force since the Internet', and a new world-view is being called upon to stem the damage that may already have been caused by the industrial sprint of the past 200 years. In this context, China is already well down the How-Fast-and-When tunnel by building large factories, industrial plants and carbon-intensive industries. India, seemingly a laggard in industrialization, still has an opportunity to ask Whether-or-Not questions.

An even more important lesson from the 'democratic experience' is the dynamics of democracy. The real fruits of democracy come when citizens 'work' their democracy, when they engage to build institutions. More than the Roosevelts and the Kennedys, it was the cattle rancher and the railroad pioneer who built the USA. Modern India and its race forward will be shaped not only in state capitals but also by the varied mini institutions across the nation. India's progress will take place not only in the halls of Parliament, but by the creation of model towships such as Tilonia, by the courage of people like Kiran Bedi, by the experiences of the submarine commander in Vizag and by the innovative factory manager at Bajaj auto.

A country starts to prosper when the people, alongside the government, start working together to build a nation. While we have a number of seemingly insurmountable problems, we have a future that is powered by the momentum of a growing country. Gerd Behrens, a reporter for *Time* magazine, draws a contrast between this passion with the attitude in more developed economies when he says the West resembles a marriage of convenience, while other growing civilizations are passionate affairs. This is relevant to India today.

Years after the event, I often had a chance to discuss the *yatra* with the rest of the group. How did they gain from it? What changed in them, and how did this impact their daily lives? A number of viewpoints emerged but two answers were consistent. First, prior to the journey, they had their own sheltered views on India. They saw India in their families, in small towns, in their schools, and for the NRI participants, from an external vantage point. After the event, they saw it as a whole – a country made up of many types of people, with different agendas, but whole nevertheless. Secondly, the participants discovered that there were others who felt positively about India. If they wanted to bring about positive change others would follow suit. Watching ordinary people do extraordinary things made the participants realize that they were not alone in their ideals.

Often in urban India, a love for your country is somehow not seen worthy of demonstration. People are trained to write cards on Mother's Day, Father's Day, birthdays, but if someone sneaks out an email with the Indian flag on the 15th August or 26th January, they can be sure it will be read with an indulgent smile. After the *yatra*, we wore our love for India on our sleeves. We were passionate about India, and when we saw that so many others had similar feelings, we felt safe in expressing it. This free expression of our love for our country is the first step in building India. Clearly, there was a segment on the train that was there to have just 'fun', but there was an equally strong and growing segment which wanted to have 'fun building India'.

Mohit Joshi, expressed his experiences during the *yatra* in Hindi: '*Sochane par kitna vichitra lagta hai ki pichle bees din hamne hilte, hilte bitaye hai. Khate waqt, sochte waqt, nahate waqt, bolte waqt, sunte waqt, nachate waqt, gaate waqt – har kaam train ki gati ke saath, hichkole khate hue. Sote to Rajasthan mein aur jaagte to Punjab mein. Dilli mein kapadon ki char tahen zaroorat hoti thi, aur Hyderabad mein garmi ke mare pasine nikal rahe the. Har bogi mein lage speaker subah subah Rahman ka vande mataram suna kar neend puri kar dete the.*'

'Upon reflection, it seems unbelievable that we spent the last twenty days constantly rocking, while eating, while thinking, while bathing, while speaking, while listening, while dancing, while singing all to the rhythm of the train in motion. We would go to sleep in Rajasthan and wake up in Punjab. In Delhi's chilly weather, we needed four layers of clothing, while in Hyderabad's heat, we would be sweating profusely. Every morning, the speakers installed in our cabin would wake us to the uplifting tunes of Rahman's *Vande Mataram*.'

Karishma Hussain recently wrote about discovering herself during the *yatra*: 'I learned a bit about myself. A lot of people thought I was "proud" and, I think elitist. I realized that I judged people as interesting based on how intelligent they were. And that has changed. I am now madly fascinated by people, not just by their intellect, which is a small part of who they are, but for the hundred shadows in their soul. I really enjoyed the company of people who were on the *yatra*. At times, I used to cringe from the constant company of people. I was trying to escape the constant hum of people! Funny as this may sound, but I'm hugely popular now in comparison to then. And I think it's because the *yatra* taught me to value people, just everyday ordinary heroes who dream, think, live, write, sleep, love, with the passion of gods.'

As our train approached Mumbai, Clyde D' Souza, a participant from Mumbai, penned the following evocative thoughts at the end to the journey:

<u>Mumbai</u>

We have reached Dombivli, so close to my immobile home;
  I am going to miss this one terribly.
I pack my bag and my mind wanders to the first day when
  I was lugging my bag around amongst strangers.
Today as I carry my bag outside, the people around me are
  not mere faces but they represent feelings, incidents,
    memories, experiences,
A whole gamut of emotions that brings 'life into existence'.

I see the evening sun in Mumbai after twenty-two days,
Just twenty-two days passed in the blink of an eye;
I've seen enchanting places and witnessed dreams turn
into realities.

The dedication of villagers in Tilonia,
The mesmerizing spiritual Golden Temple
The eternally picturesque, surreal Taj,
The ancient carvings in Ajanta, the modern day industries
of India...

If the physical journey was insightful, the mental vision
and journey was infinitely more enriching.

As the ABRY 97-98 rolls into Mumbai Central,
The train comes to a grinding halt,
The engine is turned off, the windows shut.
However, the engines in our minds are raring to go.

The train now lies stripped of its inhabitants,
Energetic voices echo in its corridors,
Water splashes in the bath,
Vande Mataram resonates in silence,
Only a golden ray of sun creeping in participates
And the future sunbeams shine on.

Our circular journey through India also reflected the return of history. 'Optimists saw history proceeding along straight lines until it hit its target, but the world moves not like an arrow, but a boomerang.' These words of Ralph Ellison reflect the cyclicality inherent in Indian philosophy where time is described as *samay chakra*, or a time wheel. Much like a googly in cricket, or the non-linear growth of Google, the industrial world was giving way to a new era of knowledge. India is already beginning to overtake the West in a number of areas. When the number of mobile phones added in India yearly exceed the total mobile phone strength in the Netherlands, when the telephone exchange recently installed in Deoria is better than that in the suburbs of London, non-linearity is here to stay.

When I first read Alvin Toffler's *Third Wave*, it opened a world of possibilities for an eighteen-year-old. I remember finishing the book in Udhampur on my way to Kashmir. In his book, Alvin Toffler, a writer and futurist, describes the coming information wave as the force that is to supercede the industrial wave that had taken over from a previous agricultural age. As we travelled the Jawahar Tunnel, under the Banihal Pass, the new possibilities that the book opened before me were reflected in the *chinar*-lined vistas of the Kashmir valley. The old industrial world of the second wave was opening up into the third wave of the knowledge era. But as time has passed, even the Tofflers have expanded their view of the Third Wave. In 1995, a few years before our journey, Alvin and Heidi Toffler redefined the Third Wave and the impact it would have on society. 'The Third Wave brings with it a genuinely new way of life based on diversified, renewable energy sources, on methods of production that make most factory assembly lines obsolete; on new, non-nuclear families... The emergent civilization writes a new code of behaviour for us and carries us beyond standardization, synchronization and centralization...'

For India the Third Wave may be defined more broadly than in the technological terms used by the Tofflers. It can be defined in terms of the service economy. So far India's visible success has been the export of services in IT and recently BPO services. But as the local economy takes off, an internal service economy can lead India's transformation. Instead of transforming from a largely agricultural economy to an industrial one, India may be the first large country that transforms into a service economy before it becomes a manufacturing power. If this is accepted as a national strategy, it requires greater effort in customization, innovation, building relationships and the underlying values of trust and integrity that our values group explored during the journey. It will also require us to realize that the mechanical replication of the West, instead of taking us forward, could slide us back.

During the journey, as we looked back on the past fifty years, we saw that while the heavy hand of the government was visible, it had focused on industrialization, leaving the knowledge and service sector to take an entrepreneurial leap forward. As we discovered India through the journey, we found it surprisingly well equipped to compete in and even define the Third Wave. Having grown up in India as citizens of a Third World country, we may be able to define ourselves over the next fifty years as the Third Wave country. We will then contribute more originally to the ideas that will shape India and the world fifty years hence.

Progress and success are a state of mind. The frame of mind we saw during our journey was one of striving and achievement. The renaissance in western Europe and the economic surge in North America were characterized by a sociological and a psychological high, as much as a material one. Much like those experiences, rarely in recent history have Indians felt so strongly that they are living in times when great opportunities beckon.

~

We reached Mumbai at 4 p.m. A massive cake had been organized to welcome the train back to Mumbai. The press had thankfully left, so the parting at the end of this twenty-two day journey was a private one. We had formed close bonds; and the journey had opened our eyes to an India we could only have imagined existed. As we asked participants to recount their favourite experiences during the journey, the visit to the Golden Temple on that drizzly December evening was on top of the list, followed closely by the experiences at Tilonia, Ralegaon Siddhi, and, interestingly, that dangerous commute at Santragachi. We had been fortunate that no major incident or injury had taken place during the journey.

Organizers and participants broke away after many a tearful hug. I had grown close to a number of facilitators and *yatris* who had become a part of the organizing group. I had personally developed a perspective that was young, informed and affected by the ideals of youth. Before I left for London, I penned a farewell note to all the participants. It reflected my state of mind – a sense of feeling drained by the effort and at the same time elevated by the passion and ideas that had surrounded me. Often, over the course of organizing the event, a voice from above had driven me on. I am personally richer as a result.

As I boarded the flight to London, I recalled the story of Naipaul, when he bade his village goodbye at the end of his first visit to India. In the first of his Indian trilogies, *An Area of Darkness*, Naipaul literally flees with relief from 'the village of the Dubes'. My village, Barpar, is only a few hundred kilometres from 'the village of the Dubes'. Barpar is named after a 200-year-old banyan tree – the village on the other side of the *bar* tree. The tree has given our family and our community shelter for 200 years of India's chequered history. It has seen off thousands of storms, hundreds of lightning strikes, not to mention years of foreign rule. It has also seen our village grow and prosper over the first fifty years of independence. As I flew out to London, I felt the tug of its many roots drawing me earthwards. I had spent several summers as a child under its thick foliage. I had only one thought as I bade farewell – to return as soon as possible.

a lightning strikes, not to mention scars of foreign rule. It has also seen our village grow and prosper over the first fifty years of independence. As I flew out to London, I felt the tug of its many roots drawing me earthwards. I had spent several summers as a child under its thick foliage. I had only one thought as I bade farewell—to return as soon as possible.

Epilogue

The *yatra* officially ended twenty-two days after it had begun. The next couple of months after the *yatra* were spent in making sure that the many tedious loose ends of the enterprise were tied up. We had some deficit in our finances, we had to make sure that an audio-visual was created for the sponsors, and we had to wind up the project office as I had to return to my job in London. Two people were extremely helpful in taking care of these details. My father-in-law, Surendra Sharma, took almost a year to make sure that back payments that the railways owed us were made. Without him and his pragmatic guidance, the *yatra* would not have have taken place, and we dedicated the audio-visual to him. In addition, Shishir Dhulla, one of the organizers, immersed himself in the task of making sure that the accounts were settled properly. Shishir continues to be an informal sounding board for the next *yatra* and his passion for India is exemplary.

In recent months we have brainstormed ideas for the next *yatra* with Milind, Mrigank, Purva, Subhashish, Mohit, Juhi, Gitanjali, Kaustav, Shishir, Angshuman and Vikrant – all participants of the first journey. Our vision for the next *yatra* is to visit modern institutions which demonstrate cases of social or economic entrepreneurship. In the process, we want to interact with individuals who have created those institutions and learn first hand the art of building. We want to interact with individuals like Narayan Murthy at Infosys, Lakshmi Mittal from Mittal Steel, and Ila Bhatt at SEWA. We hope to do a better job of publicizing this event with the help of the national media. We would like to spread the message of entrepreneurship across the country through this national adventure.

We intend to call the next journey *Jagriti Yatra*. We also aim to establish institutes for social and economic entrepreneurship to provide second-tier towns and village with practical tools and guidance for entrepreneurship. We've received initial seed funding through well-wishers, and a team is being readied to take on the project. For further information, please go to www.jagritiyatra.com.

Dr V.S. Raju talked of the *yatra* being an important 'out of class experience'. We are positioning the next *yatra* as a 'semester on wheels'. We would like IITs and other educational institutions to send their students and give them credits for it. We are in the process discussing such a 'semester' with different IITs.

When I decided to write this book, it was primarily for my growing family. Now that the book is complete, I hope that others, Indians and non-Indians alike, get something out of it. But as I re-read drafts of the book, I realized that I had often ignored the analytical for the passionate. Much like the journey, my essay to my daughters and the description of the journey merged with a description of my personal experiences. Insights gained from starting my business, from walks in my village, from my personal experiences growing up in India had influenced my thinking to a far greater extent than I had originally imagined. Much like eastern and Sufi philosophy, the observed and the observer had merged. And I do not apologize for that.

Gauri and I were the catalysts for the first *yatra*, but our job is done. We have always said that for the next *yatra*, organizers should reserve berths for us so that we can travel as facilitators with our children in tow. People from the last *yatra* or from our wide circle of friends will have to come forward to take charge and get the next *yatra* going. Our aim remains to make it a sustainable event that takes place perhaps once every year.

I rest my pen with that challenge. This narrative has been long overdue, but it needed the onset of the sixtieth anniversary of India's independence to get it going. The framework for this book was completed over the course of forty-eight hours in Kanyakumari on 15 August 2004. At the stroke of midnight on that windy night, I swam out to sea at the southernmost tip of India, alone with these thoughts.

The Yatris

Vikrant did his master's in Management from the Tata Institute of Social Sciences (TISS) Mumbai. He works for Novartis and is married to a captain in the Indian Army. Together, they organize an annual lecture for his grandfather – the Gandhian who was his inspiration.

Purva pursued dentistry in Mumbai. She won the *Competition Success Review* Miss India contest in 2002. She travelled to compete for the Miss India title in San Francisco, no doubt pinning Indian flags on every passerby.

Devang, after graduating from Guy's and Thomas' Hospital in London, decided to join the British Navy as a doctor. He is married and lives in Portsmouth, UK. He has recently served in Iraq.

Karthikeyan keeps in touch with me through his annual greeting cards on 15th August. To the best of my knowledge, he continues to work as a teacher in Tamil Nadu.

Milind has worked in the software industry in India and Europe. After completing his MBA from Oxford University, he now works with the consulting firm Booz Allen & Hamilton in London. Milind is one of the key people involved in organizing the next *yatra*.

Mohit went to Hindu College in Delhi to pursue a degree in economics, and then went to do an MBA from IIM Lucknow. He now works with the HSBC in Delhi. He continues to read Ayn Rand and enjoys listening to Kishore Kumar songs.

Karthik completed his engineering course in Mumbai and got a scholarship to Georgetown University in Washington D.C. to do his MBA. He is currently completing his PhD at the Massachusetts Institute of Technology in Boston.

Gitanjali completed her studies at the Wildlife Institute of India, Dehra Dun. She is currently completing her PhD from Columbia University on the Indian rhinoceros, with extensive and often dangerous field work in Kaziranga and Jaldapara sanctuaries.

Angshuman followed his passion for journalism. At present, he is a successful journalist in Kolkata. I know that wherever he is people will wake up to exciting news.

Juhi followed her heart and went on to do her master's from the National Institute of Design, Ahmedabad. She works for a design company in Mumbai.

Radheyshyam used to write to the other *yatris* and to Gitanjali in particular. We are not sure where he is now. Although, if he chances upon this book, I request him to get in touch.

Subhashish or Shark graduated from IIT Chennai and attended IIM Ahmedabad to do his MBA. He has worked with different IT service companies and is currently with Accenture in Australia, helping generate support from IITs for future *yatras*.

Raghav continues to work in Australia, and no amount of corporate life will take the maverick out of him. His sense of curiosity, adventure, childlike innocence, combined with a risqué sense of humour, continues to regale us.

Raju Bhaiya still works as a senior manager at Grameen Bank, Gorakhpur. His two sons have inherited their father's enthusiasm, and we hope as young college-going students, they will take part in the next *yatra*. I know, I will not be able to keep Raju Bhaiya away even if I tried.

Frank continues to live in his houseboat in the Little Venice region of London. Our documentary still remains unmade.

Acknowledgements

I got enormous support while writing the book from Chitra Sundaram, Udayan and Anuja Kelkar, Tushar and Rewati Prabhu, Ushma and John Williams, Kirstin McIntosh, Madhuvanti Ghose, Helen Owers, Gitanjali and Kaustav Bhattacharya, Milind Singh, Mohit Joshi, Mrigank Tripathi, Subhashish Sarkar, Vikrant Bhuskute, and Smriti Kedia. I would also like to thank numerous other participants from the *yatra* who shared anecdotes over the phone and through their written comments.

A number of individuals at HarperCollins Publishers India deserve credit for bringing this story to the reader. I would like to thank Mr P.M. Sukumar for believing in the book; and Krishan Chopra for his help at a key point in the editing process.

I would like to thank my father Lieutenant General Shri Prakash Mani (retired) who first inspired to me to discover India; my mother, Shashi, who runs a vocational training organization, with emphasis on skill development and women's empowerment, and is an inspiration for the whole family. My sister, Shipra is by far the strongest person in the family and helped organize the *yatra*. She, along with my brother Mrigank, will be a major force in the ones to come.

A group of us ten fellow IITians from Delhi lived together for four years and had experiences that can only be described as mad. That bond of madness keeps us together, and strangely keeps us sane. The context of the journey would be very different without Vineet Khosla, Raghav Mehra, Rahul Dhir, Umesh Baveja, Rohit Bhagat, Udayan Kelkar, Samir Seth, Pawan Rewari, Ram Challa and Rajiv Arora.

The idea of the *yatra* was hatched in the environs of the International Management Institute Lausanne in 1995. My eighty-odd classmates continued to give me ideas that made the journey international and not limited to India alone.

In conceptualizing and implementing the journey, I would particularly like to thank Azad Shivdasani, who was one of the first to believe in the concept. He provided financial support and saw the project through to completion. Raju Shete, a successful entrepreneur, took to the concept and helped us in Mumbai. Madhur Bajaj, who has been a friend and guide, provided enormous encouragement, often involving the entire Bajaj family. Vikram Sakhuja was a constructive critic and at the crunch point, a huge supporter. Madhuvanti Ghose, descends from a family of freedom fighters, and helped us conceptualize the *yatra*. Steven Yurisich grasped the idea quickly and made the journey international.

In India, Ambika Srivastava was the first to believe in the journey. Deepali Pahwa was an enormous help before, during and after the *yatra.* Raghav Mehra was there when I needed him most. Kirti Panchal kept the faith when it mattered most. My father-in-law, Surendra Sharma, was pivotal in providing support that formed the backbone of the project.

I will always be grateful for the unconditional support of Shri Basu Bhattacharya (Basu Da), Snehlata Maheshwari (Nani Ma) and Dr Vidya Niwas Mishra (Babuji) who are no longer with us.

And finally, my thoughts turn to our elder daughter Tarini who was born a month after the journey was completed. She was delivered underweight. We think this was a result of the strains Gauri suffered while organizing the journey. She has grown to be the tallest girl in her class, and we no longer have those concerns. I hope as Tarini grows, she receives some intellectual nourishment from this book that we may have otherwise failed to provide.

I would also like to thank the Indian Railways, Yuvak Biradari (Bharat), The Inlaks Foundation, Coca-Cola India, Colgate India, HRD Ministry (Golden Jubilee Committee), Hutch, Motorola India, Godrej Foundation, IIT (Mumbai), Vikram Sarabhai Space Centre, Sabarmati Ashram, The President's Bodyguard, IIT (Delhi), King George Medical College (Lucknow), Tata Steel (Jamshedpur), The National Museum (Kolkata), Eastern Naval Command Visakhapatnam, Armoured Corps Centre and School (Ahmednagar), Bajaj Auto (Aurangabad), National Defence Academy (Pune), Travel Corporation of India (Mumbai).

A special thanks to: Jaya Bachchan, Kiran Bedi, Neera Benegal, Shyam Benegal, Benoy Behl, Suraj Bhan, Bharat Bala, Veena Bhargava, S.R. Bommai, Rahul Bose, Pandit Hari Prasad Chaurasia, General M.L. Chibber, Hutokshi Doctor, Ram Gidoomal, Pheroza Godrej, S.P. Godrej, Anna Hazare, Ramkrishan Hinduja, Sadiq Imam, Darshana Jhaveri, Siddharth Kak, Sanjana Kapoor, Adi Katghara, Riz Khan, Maitrey Kumar, Adrian Lajtha, Sunil Lulla, Lieutenant General Shamsher Mehta, Kanika Meyer, Ashok Misra, Arun Nanda, N. Nandakumara, Rajendra Pachauri, Nani Palkhivala, Jagdish Parikh, Avinash Pasricha, Madho Pathak, Lieutenant General Sushil Pillai, Jerry Pinto, Rashmi Poddar, Ravi Reddy, Julius Ribeiro, Bunker Roy, Gautam Sen, Kranti Shah, Devendra Sharma, Ramendra Sharma, Indra Dev Sharma, Arvind Sikand, Ajit Singh, Lakshmi

Mall Singhvi, Suhas Sukhatme, C.P. Tripathi, Shri Vilas Mani Tripathi, Dhananjaya Tripathi, Mark Tully, Dina Vakil, Lieutenant General J.S. Verma.

I would like to thank those who helped in making the journey possible: Vandana Agarwal, Mayassa Al Malazi, Rajeev Singh Arora, Sandeep Bahanda, Vijay Bahiti, Geeta Bajaj, Umesh Baveja, Dev Benegal, Rohit Bhagat, Avinishka Bhattacharya, Jimmy Billimoria, Kamal Chaube, Ranjit Das, Shomilyo Datta, Sangeeta Datta, Vasanth Davis, Mike Denzel, Rahul Dhir, Shishir Dhulla, Rashmi Dickinson, Edward Dickinson, Dhananjaya Divekar, Medha Divekar, Paul East, David Fisher, Rajiv Gupta, Sanjeev Gupta, Anita Horam, Tariq Hussain, Cyrus Hoshidar, Shireen Issal, Keith Jackson, Bridget Jackson, Pavan Kapoor, Homi Katghara, Ashish Khaitan, Seema Khanna, Somesh Khanna, Vineet Khosla, Monish Mahurkar, Padmini Mahurkar, Pramod Malviya, Siddharth Mande, Purnima Mane, Ashish Mittal, Perzon Mody, Munir Mohanty, Karthik Muralidharan, Shankar Narain, Badri Nathan, Sangitika Nigam, Veenu Pasricha, Colonel Suresh Patil, Anthony Paul, Ameet Phadnis, Praveena V., Hosla Prasad, Satish Raheja, Vrinda Rajgarhia, Sandeep Reddy, Harjeet Singh Rekhi, Shefali Rekhi, Pawan Rewari, Sumit Roy, Ajay Sahani, Simmi Sakhuja, Vipul Sangoi, Amita Sarwal, John Sequeira, Samir Seth, Anjya Seth, Kumar Shah, Anshuman Sharma, Padma Sharma, Archana Sharma, Dhruv Sharma, Sanjay Sharma, Aradhna Sharma, Ameet Shah, Vijay Shukla, Rajeev Shukla, Swati Shukla, Rameshwar Singh, Robert Skelton, Hilary Smith, Rajat Somani, Nandit Soparkar, Malini Suri, Rachna Swarup, Kalpana Talwar, Anuradha Tarafdar, Ashok Thomas, Prashant Tiwari, Frank Worth.

Bibliography

Ballow, John J., Robert J. Thomas and Göran Roos, 'Future Value: The $7 Trillion Challenge'. *Journal of Applied Corporate Finance,* Volume 16, December 2004.

Bernstein, William. *The Birth of Plenty*. McGraw Hill, 2004.

Bhagat, Chetan. *Five Point Someone – What Not to Do at IIT*, Rupa & Co., 2004

Boorstin, Daniel J. *The Americans: The Democratic Experience*. Vintage, 1974.

Braudel, Fernand. *History of Civilizations*. Penguin Viking, 1993.

Bryson, Bill. *A Short History of Nearly Everything*. Broadway, 2003.

Capra, Fritjof. *The Tao of Physics,* Simon & Schuster, 1982.

Cheng'en, Wu, W.J.F. Jenner. *Journey to the West*. Foreign Language Press, 2003.

Collins, Jim. *Good to Great*. HarperCollins Publishers, 2001.

Das, Gurcharan. *India Unbound*. Penguin Books India, 2002.

Dreze, Jean and Amartya Sen. *India: Economic Development and Social Opportunity*. Oxford University Press, 1998.

Dyson, Tim, Robert Cassen and Leela Visaria. *Twenty First Century India: Population, Economy, Human Development and the Environment*. Oxford University Press, 2004.

Eley, Geoff and Ronald Grigor Suny. *Becoming National: A Reader*. Oxford University Press, 1996.

Enriquez, Juan. *As the Future Catches You*. Crown Business, 2001.

Fernandez-Armesto, Felipe. *Millennium.* Free Press, 1996.

Friedman, Thomas. *The Lexus and the Olive Tree: Understanding Globalization.* Farrar, Straus and Giroux, 2000.

Gandhi, M.K. *The Story of My Experiments with Truth*. Penguin Books India, 1982.

Huang, Yasheng and Tarun Khanna. 'Can India Overtake China'. *Foreign Policy*, July-August, 2003.

Huntington, Samuel. *Who Are We?.* Simon & Schuster, 2004.

Huntington, Samuel. *The Clash of Civilizations and Remaking of World Order*. Simon & Schuster, 1998.

Iyengar, B.K.S. *Light on the Yoga Sutras of Patanjali*. HarperCollins Publishers India, 1993.

Jalan, Bimal. *The Future of India: Politics, Economics and Governance*. Penguin Books India, 2005.

Kalam, A.P.J. Abdul and Arun Tiwari. *Wings of Fire: An Autobiography of A.P.J Abdul Kalam*. Sangam Books, 1999.

Keay, John. *India, a History.* HarperCollins Publishers, 2001.

Lala, R.M. *For the Love of India: The Life and Times of Jamsetji Tata*. Penguin Books India, 2004.

Mehta, Suketu. 'Welcome to Bollywood', *National Geographic*, February, 2005.

Naipaul, V.S. *India – A Million Mutinies Now*. Penguin, 1992.

Naipaul, V.S. *India – A Wounded Civilization*. Vintage, 2003.

New Delhi Foreign Institute. *Planning Commission's Report of the Committee on India Vision 2020*, Academic Foundation, 2003.

Rostow, Walt D. *The Stages of Economic Growth: A Non-Communist Manifesto.* Cambridge University Press, 1971.

Sankrityayan, Rahul. *Volga Se Ganga.* Kitab Mahal, 1942.

Sen, Amartya. *Development as Freedom*. Anchor Books, 2000.

Sheshabalaya, Ashutosh. *Rising Elephant – The Growing Clash with India Over White-collar Jobs and its Challenge to America and the World*. Common Courage Press, 2004.

Subramaniam, T.S.R. *Journeys through Babudom and Netaland*, Rupa & Co., 2004

Toffler, Alvin and Heidi Toffler. *Creating a New Civilization*. Turner Publishing Inc., 1995.

Toynbee, Arnold. *Half the World: The History and Culture of China and Japan.* Holt, Rinehart and Winston, 1973.

Toynbee, Arnold. *A Study of History.* Oxford University Press, 1957.

Trevelyan, G.O. *The Life and Letters of Lord Macaulay*. Longmans Green, 1881.

Index